P9-CFU-793

GAME DAY
YANKEES BASEBALL

GAME DAY
YANKEES BASEBALL

**The Greatest Games, Players, Managers and Teams
in the Glorious Tradition of Yankees Baseball**

TRIUMPH
B O O K S
CHICAGO

AMERICA'S PREMIER SPORTS ANNUALS

Copyright © 2006 by Athlon Sports and Triumph Books

No part of this publication may be reproduced, stored in a retrieval system, or transmitted, in any form by any means, electronic, mechanical, photocopying, or otherwise, without the prior written permission of the publisher, Triumph Books, 542 S. Dearborn St., Suite 750, Chicago, Illinois 60605.

Library of Congress Control Number: 2005910953

This book is available in quantity at special discounts for your group or organization.
For further information, contact:

Triumph Books
542 South Dearborn Street
Suite 750
Chicago, Illinois 60605
(312) 939-3330
Fax (312) 663-3557

WRITER: Tyler Kepner

EDITORS: Rob Doster, Mitchell Light

PHOTO EDITOR: Tim Clark

DESIGN: Anderson Thomas Design

PHOTO CREDITS: Getty Images, AP/Wide World, Hulton Archive, Major League Baseball, National Baseball Hall of Fame, Time Life Pictures, Steve Moore

Printed in U.S.A.

ISBN-13: 978-1-57243-835-4
ISBN-10: 1-57243-835-5

CONTENTS

Foreword

People always ask me if I believe in "Yankee luck." I don't know, but I always felt pretty lucky being a Yankee.

My old manager Casey Stengel used to say there's something inspiring about putting on a Yankees uniform, and I believed that to be true. I believed it when I first joined the Yankees, during the last two weeks of the 1946 season. I was a 21-year-old kid, just called up from Newark, in the same locker room as DiMaggio, Henrich, Keller, Rizzuto, all those guys. You saw the way they acted—dedicated, proud, professional. As I came to know, that was the Yankee way. Mostly I came to know it wasn't just having great players; it was having great teams. DiMaggio was probably the best player I ever played with. He did everything so surely, so skillfully, but nothing mattered to him unless the team won. If he didn't think you were bearing down, giving it your all, God help you.

We had a real team spirit on the Yankees, everybody pulling for each other. Winning those five straight championships from 1949 to 1953, that took pretty good pulling together. In those days, lots of people hated the Yankees.

They complained we won too much. All I can say is, too bad.

Whenever I look at those old pictures in our museum at Montclair State University, I remember how much we were like family. I was lucky to play with guys like Mickey Mantle, Ellie Howard, Whitey Ford, Roger Maris, Moose Skowron, Bobby Richardson and Tony Kubek. We all had a bond and looked out for each other. We did everything together, whether playing cards on the train or going out to the movies. We were all friends.

To me, Yankee Stadium is still a shrine—it's changed, but it's the same because there's a lot of respect in the place. When out-of-towners come to New York, they want to see the Statue of Liberty and Yankee Stadium. I think the players there today, they realize they're part of a great heritage—they're surrounded by it. Going into the clubhouse you pass all those pictures of Ruth and Gehrig and Dickey and Mantle and Munson. That's a pretty good reminder. The Yankees are the only team that still holds Old-Timers Day; they celebrate their history. And in spring training, they bring back guys like me, Whitey, Reggie and Nettles to be around to help.

If you ask me, the Yankees are different. They're a lot like New York: lots of energy, lots of expectations. Maybe there is something about the pinstripes. I think when you're a Yankee, anything is possible.

—YOGI BERRA

Johnny Mize, ca. 1950

Introduction

The images are unforgettable and too numerous to count.

Babe Ruth swatting majestic home runs into the New York sky. Lou Gehrig gracing the game with quiet dignity and unparalleled excellence. Joe DiMaggio capturing the imagination of an entire nation with his effortless greatness. Mickey Mantle, beloved by a generation of boys inspired to pick up a bat and glove to emulate their idol, thrilling fans with his power. Reggie Jackson and Derek Jeter, two of the dominant postseason performers in baseball history, making history on the sport's biggest stage.

We're taking the history, drama and pageantry of Yankees baseball and distilling them into the pages that follow. It's a daunting task. No professional franchise in all of sports inspire the loyalty and passion—and yes, the hatred—that the Yankees elicit from baseball fans, and with good reason.

Through the words and images we present, we hope you will get a taste of what the New York Yankees are all about. Decades have passed since players first donned the pinstripes, but one thing hasn't changed: Yankees baseball is an unmatched tradition, a legacy of greatness, a way of life.

TRADITIONS AND PAGEANTRY

The sights and sounds of Game Day in The Bronx create an unmatched spectacle, a glorious mix of tradition and color and pomp and pageantry. Here's a small sample of what makes the New York Yankees unique among all professional sports franchises.

The Name

The Yankees franchise began ingloriously. The Baltimore Orioles folded after just two seasons, and they were sold to Frank Farrell and Bill Devery for $18,000 before the 1903 season. The team was nicknamed the Highlanders after its home field, Hilltop Park,

which was constructed in just six weeks at 168th Street and Broadway, one of the highest points in the city. When they moved to the Polo Grounds in 1913, the franchise dropped the name Highlanders and officially adopted Yankees, as it had been referred to in newspaper headlines as far back as 1904.

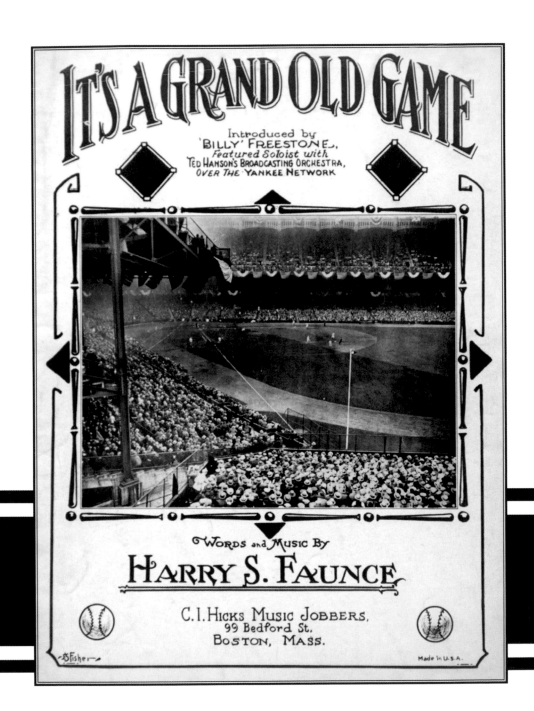

Yankee Stadium

The drawing power of Babe Ruth was so great that it got the Yankees evicted from the Polo Grounds. The Giants had let the Yankees share their home since 1913, but when Ruth arrived in 1920, he made the Yankees a more popular draw, and the Giants kicked them out. The Yankees' owners, Jacob Ruppert and Tillinghast L'Hommedieu Huston, wasted no time in building a $2.5 million palace of their own, directly across the Harlem River from

the Polo Grounds. It was the first facility to be called a stadium, and it seated 58,000. There were quirky dimensions: a 395-foot power alley in left field, a 460-foot mark in deep left center, and a cozy 295-foot distance to the right field foul pole. It truly seemed to be the House That Ruth Built. An extensive remodeling in 1974 and '75 brought about a new championship era at Yankee Stadium, where Reggie Jackson, Derek Jeter and others would carry on Ruth's tradition. In addition to all the baseball, Yankee Stadium was the home field of the NFL Giants from 1956 through 1973 and the

New York Cosmos soccer team in the 1960s and '70s. The park has hosted 30 championship fights, concerts by U2, Billy Joel and Pink Floyd and two papal masses. In June 2005, the Yankees announced plans to privately finance a new Yankee Stadium, at a cost of $800 million, to be opened in 2009 across 161st Street from the current ballpark. The team plans to preserve the Yankee Stadium field and incorporate more elements of the pre-1976 ballpark into the new one, including the façade around the rim of the stadium.

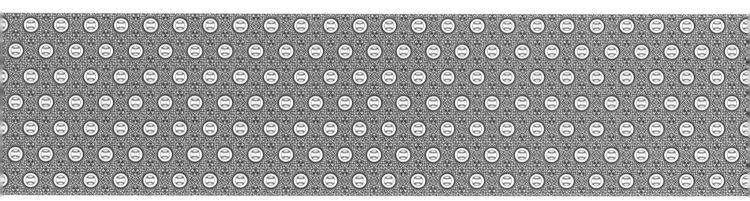

Monument Park

Before Yankee Stadium was remodeled in the 1970s, the Yankees allowed fans to leave the ballpark through the center field gate, which gave them a chance to look at the monuments honoring legends of the past. Now, fans line up before the game to tour Monument Park, located a long home run away from the plate beside the bullpens beyond center field. The first monument, erected in 1932, honored the late Manager Miller Huggins. It was located in the field of play, as were the monuments for Lou Gehrig and Babe Ruth. Since the remodeling, the Yankees have dedicated three other monuments, to Mickey Mantle, Joe DiMaggio and the victims of the Sept. 11, 2001 attacks. In addition, 20 plaques honoring past Yankee greats line the walls at Monument Park.

Bob Sheppard

Since April 17, 1951, the unmistakable voice of Bob Sheppard—also known as "The Voice of God"—has wafted over generations of fans at Yankee Stadium. Sheppard's first Yankees lineup included Joe DiMaggio, Phil Rizzuto, Yogi Berra and Mickey Mantle, whose name, he has said, is his favorite of all to announce.

(The second is Shigetoshi Hasegawa, a reliever for Anaheim and Seattle.) More than 50 years after his debut, Sheppard, who is coy about his age, still ventured to the clubhouses to ask players for the proper pronunciations of their names. In 2000, he donated his Stadium microphone to the Hall of Fame.

Pinstripes and the Interlocking NY

Pinstripes might be thinning, but the Yankees did not start wearing them to flatter a portly Babe Ruth. According to the Baseball Hall of Fame, the Yankees actually first donned pinstripes in 1912. They did not wear them the next two seasons, but have done so every year since 1915. Ruth, of course, did not join the team until 1920. His uniforms never had

the famous interlocking NY on the left breast, a feature that did not become a permanent part of the uniform until 1936. The logo has appeared on the caps ever since 1922 and originated from an 1877 design for a medal given by the New York Police Department to Officer John McDowell, the first New York City policeman to be shot in the line of duty.

—— Retired Numbers ——

The Yankees were the first team to wear uniform numbers, with the 1929 team assigned numbers based on their spots in the batting order. Babe Ruth batted third and wore No. 3, Lou Gehrig batted fourth and wore No. 4, and so on. Gehrig's number was retired in 1939, and since then 15 other players and managers have had their numbers retired, with Bill Dickey and Yogi Berra both honored for No. 8. The numbers are displayed beyond the left-centerfield wall at the entrance to Monument Park at Yankee Stadium. The next number to be retired will likely be Paul O'Neill's No. 21, which has not been issued since O'Neill retired after the 2001 season.

——— No Beards ———

George Steinbrenner attended the Culver Military Academy and has tried to bring the same sense of discipline to the Yankees since buying the team in 1973. If Steinbrenner had his way, every player would have a crew-cut. As it is, he gets his point across by forbidding long hair and any facial hair besides a mustache. Players new to the Yankees know that the first thing they must do upon arriving in the clubhouse is to grab a razor. For the salaries Steinbrenner gives, players like Jason Giambi and Roger Clemens have happily obliged.

——— God Bless America ———

Since the terrorist attacks of Sept. 11, 2001, the Yankees have paused every game during the seventh inning stretch for the playing of "God Bless America." No other team observes this tradition at every game, and all of the uniformed Yankees are required to stand on the top step of the dugout, as they are before every game for "The Star-Spangled Banner." At times, "God Bless America" has seemed to give the Yankees an edge on the field. In the 2003 division series, the Minnesota Twins cited the extra delay before the bottom of the seventh as a reason that their starter, Brad Radke, came apart in the inning.

— Roll Call, Two-Strike Cheering, and Ol' Blue Eyes —

During the first few pitches of every game at Yankee Stadium, the fans in the right-centerfield bleachers chant the names of each Yankee player on the field, besides the starting pitcher (David Wells was an exception). The fans repeat the chants ("De-Rek-Je-Ter! De-Rek-Je-Ter!") until the player recognizes them with a wave or a raised glove. The fans also cheer and sometimes rise whenever a Yankees pitcher gets to two strikes, anticipating a strikeout. At the end of every Yankees victory, the public-address system plays "New York, New York," over and over as the crowd files out. It is almost always the Frank Sinatra version, though Liza Minelli gets occasional airtime after victories and always after losses.

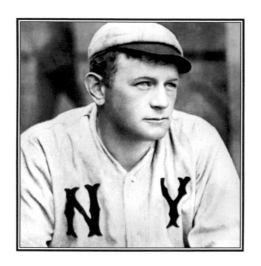

THE GREAT YANKEES

The list of great Yankees reads like a Reader's Digest guide to the Hall of Fame. The names are known to all fans of America's pastime, and for Yankee haters, they still bring a shiver of dread.

Hall of Famers

JACK CHESBRO

A master of the spitball, Chesbro was the first man to throw a pitch for the New York Highlanders, starting their inaugural game at Washington on April 22, 1903. The team that would later be known as Yankees lost, 3–1, but Chesbro would soon define his brief New York career by winning at a phenomenal rate. A 28-game winner for Pittsburgh in 1902, Chesbro would go 21–15 in 1903 and then

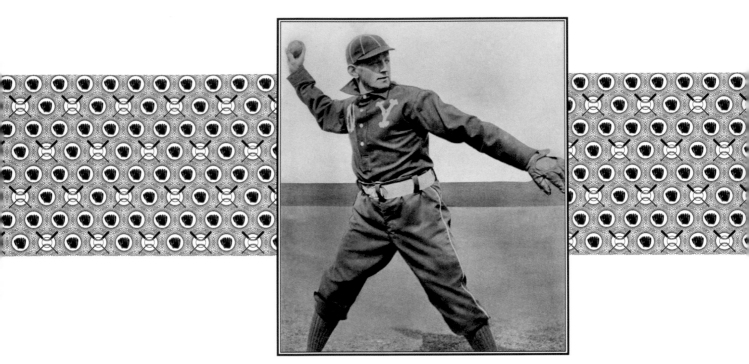

41–12 with a 1.82 ERA in 1904. His numbers that season are mind-bending: 55 games, 48 complete games, 454 2/3 innings, 338 hits allowed. Chesbro was out of baseball by the end of the decade, but he remains the only Yankees pitcher to exceed 27 victories in a season and joined the Hall of Fame posthumously, in 1946.

BABE RUTH

The Babe's monument at Yankee Stadium says it all: "A Great Ball Player, a Great Man, A Great American." Ruth truly was great, in every sense of the word. There is no bigger name in baseball history than his. He is credited with both revolutionizing the game and all but saving it after the Black Sox scandal in 1919. That was his final year with the Boston Red Sox, who sold him to the Yankees and regretted it for nearly a century. Twice a 20-game winner for the Red Sox, Ruth had become mainly a hitter in 1919, when his 29 homers set a single-season record, beating the old mark by two. In his first Yankees season, Ruth set another home run record—with 54. He broke it again, twice, swatting 60 in the storied 1927 season. His feats and appetites were so heroic that a new adjective, Ruthian, entered the vernacular. An outsized personality who made time for fans young and old, Ruth fundamentally changed the game forever. He was a showman of the highest order who excelled in the World Series, ushering in the Yankees' decades of dominance and captivating the world with his 714 home runs. The fascination with the man and the power game he created has never really ended.

WAITE HOYT

Eleven months after selling Babe Ruth to the Yankees, the Red Sox shipped Hoyt to New York on Dec. 15, 1920, as part of an eight-player trade. Hoyt, who was 10–12 in two seasons with Boston, promptly won 19 games in each of his first two Yankee seasons and went on to be a two-time 20-game winner and the ace of the staff for the 1927 and 1928 champs. When he wasn't starting, he was coming out of the bullpen, with a league-leading 8 saves in '28. Only Whitey Ford has more career starts in the World Series than Hoyt's 11. Hoyt pitched for five other teams, with limited success, after the Yankees traded him in 1930, but his heroics in pinstripes earned him a place in Cooperstown in 1969.

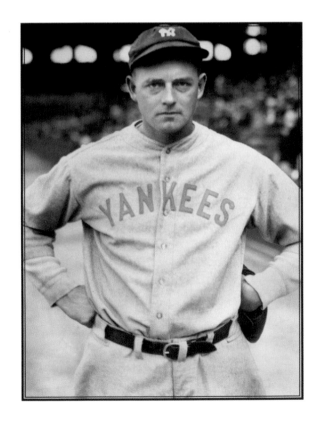

HERB PENNOCK

In 1923, the always-generous Boston Red Sox shipped Pennock, an 11-year veteran coming off a 17-loss season, to the Yankees for three middling players and $50,000. Once again, the Yankees pulled off a steal. Pennock, a savvy lefthander from Pennsylvania nicknamed "The Knight of Kennett Square," went 19–6 in his first Yankees season, culminating in a victory in the sixth game of the 1923 World Series, clinching the team's first title. A control specialist, Pennock recorded few strikeouts but rarely walked a batter. He went 240–162 with a 3.60 ERA and was named to the Hall of Fame in 1948. At the time of his death, also in 1948, he was the general manager of his hometown team, the Philadelphia Phillies.

LOU GEHRIG

Only Lou Gehrig, it seems, could retire from baseball, facing a deadly disease that would cut him down in the prime of his life, and tell 62,000 fans that he considered himself the luckiest man on the face of the earth. Gehrig's poignant, elegant address at Yankee Stadium on July 4, 1939, is as much a part of his legacy as his possibly unparalleled excellence at the plate. Gehrig and Babe Ruth formed the most devastating hitting tandem in baseball history, establishing the Yankees as the most storied franchise in sports. He hit .361 in seven World Series, winning six, and hit .340 for his career—with five seasons of 40 home runs, seven seasons of 150 runs batted in and eight seasons of 200 hits. The humble Gehrig attended Columbia University and stood in contrast to Ruth, whose earthy charm and everyman appetites made him the hero of the masses. Gehrig was a monument to toughness, playing in 2,130 consecutive games, and only his illness, which later came to bear his name, ended the streak. Gehrig was enshrined in Cooperstown in 1939—the writers waived the mandatory five-year waiting period—and he died on June 2, 1941, just shy of his 38th birthday.

EARLE COMBS

With Babe Ruth and Lou Gehrig in the middle of the Yankees' order, someone had to score all those runs. That someone was Earle Combs, a truly elite offensive player. The first in the line of great Yankee center fielders, Combs averaged 125 runs scored per season from 1925 through 1932. He was the leadoff hitter on the 1927 Yankees, leading the league in hits with 231, and he batted .350 in four World Series appearances. Known as "The Kentucky Colonel," Combs was elected to the Hall of Fame by the Veterans Committee in 1970, six years before his death.

TONY LAZZERI

A decade before Joe DiMaggio came from San Francisco to alight on the Bronx stage, Lazzeri paved the way for him. Born in San Francisco in 1903, Lazzeri joined the Yankees in 1926 and drove in 114 runs as a rookie, though his season ended with a bases-loaded strikeout against Grover Cleveland Alexander in Game 7 of the World Series, which the Yankees lost. Lazzeri would have many more chances, winning five titles as a steady run producer. Nicknamed "Poosh-Em-Up Tony," he became the first player to belt two grand slams in a game on May 24, 1936. He joined his many teammates in the Hall of Fame in 1991, 45 years after his death.

BILL DICKEY

In a glorious 17-year Yankees career, Dickey was a rock behind the plate and a model of consistency as a hitter. He caught more than 100 games for 13 seasons in a row (1929 through 1941) and batted .300 or better in 10 of his first 11 full seasons. He almost never struck out, fanning just 289 times while drawing 678 career walks. A leader on seven Yankees championship teams, Dickey managed the Yankees in his final year as a player, 1946. He later coached for the team, helping a star catching pupil named Yogi Berra carry on his tradition of catching excellence. The Yankees retired No. 8 for both Dickey and Berra in 1972.

LEFTY GOMEZ

The next time you're watching the All-Star Game, think of Lefty Gomez, the Yankee who not only won the first such game, in 1933, but also drove in the first run. Vernon Louis Gomez, nicknamed "Goofy," dazzled his teammates with his wit. Gomez claimed he talked to the baseball many times in his career. "I yelled, 'Go foul! Go foul!'" he said. But there was a serious side to Gomez on the mound. A four-time 20-game winner, Gomez won the pitching Triple Crown in 1934, leading the league in victories (26), ERA (2.33) and strikeouts (158) and in 1937 (21 wins, 2.93 ERA, 194 strikeouts). He formed half of the Yankees' brilliant lefty-righty pitching tandem, with Red Ruffing, that dominated the 1930s. Gomez went 6–0 in the World Series, helping the Yankees win five titles.

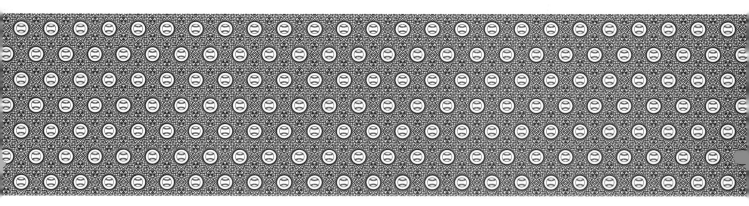

RED RUFFING

In 1928 and 1929, Ruffing lost 47 games for the Boston Red Sox. So in 1930, when the Yankees offered $50,000 and backup outfielder Cedric Durst for Ruffing, the Red Sox took the bait. Ruffing promptly turned into a Hall of Famer in pinstripes. A four-time 20-game winner for the Yankees, Ruffing went 82–33 in the championship seasons of 1936 through 1939 and compiled a 7–2 record in the World Series. He was also a fine hitter, with 36 career home runs. In 2004, 18 years after his death, the Yankees honored Ruffing with a plaque at Monument Park. "This means as much as his induction into the Hall of Fame," said his son, Charles Ruffing, Jr. "You had to live with my dad all those years to know just how much it would mean to him to be out there with his teammates."

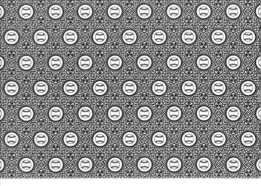

JOE DIMAGGIO

The son of a San Francisco fisherman, Joe DiMaggio became an icon of the 20th century. "Joe DiMaggio was the greatest all-around player I ever saw," said his rival of the 1940s, Ted Williams. The Yankee Clipper was that, and so much more. He may have been as much of a celebrity after his 13-year career as he was during it. DiMaggio married Marilyn Monroe in 1954 and cultivated such an air of royalty until his 1999 death that even Alex Rodriguez, who was by then a star in the major leagues, could not summon the nerve to introduce himself when he saw DiMaggio in public in the late 1990s. DiMaggio owns perhaps the most remarkable record in baseball history, a 56-game hitting streak in 1941, the second of his three MVP seasons. He led the Yankees to nine titles, including four in a row at the start of his career, from 1936 through 1939, and he made the All-Star team every year he played. DiMaggio hit .325 for his career, with 361 home runs and just 369 strikeouts, and held the unofficial title of Greatest Living Player until his death in 1999.

PHIL RIZZUTO

One generation knew Rizzuto as a scrappy shortstop who played in nine World Series for the Yankees, winning seven. The next knew him as a folksy, friendly broadcaster known for calling people "huckleberries" and exclaiming, "Holy Cow!" Rizzuto, a Brooklyn native known as "Scooter," joined the Yankees in 1941 and hit .307, one of his two seasons above .300. The other was 1950, when he batted .324—with 200 hits, 92 walks and 125 runs scored—to win the MVP award. Finally named to the Hall of Fame by the veterans committee in 1994, Rizzuto delighted the crowd on a sticky day in Cooperstown, swatting flies as he gave a rollicking, rambling speech. It was also heartfelt. Said Rizzuto that day, "I had the most wonderful lifetime any man can possibly have. And I thank you for this wonderful game they call baseball."

YOGI BERRA

The Yankees, of course, have the most world championships, with 26. The Cardinals have the next most, with 9. How would history have changed if St. Louis had considered Yogi Berra a better catching prospect than his buddy, Joe Garagiola? The Cardinals scouted both local players, but when they offered Garagiola more money, Berra rejected his hometown team to sign with the Yankees. He became, perhaps, the greatest catcher ever, winning three MVP awards and playing for 10 championship teams—more than any other player in baseball history. A legendary character of the game, Berra's many words of wisdom have become a part of the American lexicon, none more memorable than, "It ain't over til it's over." He made the All-Star team every year from 1948 through 1962, managed the Yankees to the World Series in '64, and by his 80th birthday, in 2005, he was still active as an author, a TV pitchman, a spring training coach and a trusted adviser to Yankees manager Joe Torre.

WHITEY FORD

Whitey Ford was 21 years old, coming off a 9–1 rookie season, when he beat the Phillies in Game 4 of the 1950 World Series, completing a Yankees sweep. The New York native served in the Korean War the next two years, but when Yankees fans saw him again, Ford picked up where he'd left off. He went 18–6 in 1953 to help the Yankees win another title, and went on to become the career leader in nearly every World Series pitching category (though he never started a Game 7). Known as "The Chairman of the Board," Ford had a sensational .690 career winning percentage and, in 16 seasons, he never had an ERA above 3.24. A crafty control artist, Ford is the Yankees' career leader in victories, with 236, and also tops the list in strikeouts, innings and shutouts.

MICKEY MANTLE

If Mickey Mantle's name had five syllables instead of four, he would have been named in the famous Paul Simon lyric, "Where have you gone, Joe DiMaggio?" Mantle, after all, replaced DiMaggio as the Yankees' center fielder and also achieved a hero's status in the American consciousness. Mantle was the idol of millions in the 1950s: the all-around natural, the country kid from Oklahoma who captivated the boys and made the girls swoon. Even constant injuries and a fast-paced night-life could not keep Mantle from winning seven World Series titles, three MVP awards and the 1956 Triple Crown. A prolific switch-hitter with natural power, Mantle saw his speed suffer after tearing his knee as a rookie in the 1951 World Series, catching his spikes on an exposed drain while chasing a fly ball. He more than made up for it with 536 home runs, a .298 career average, and a grip on a whole generation.

CATFISH HUNTER

The signing of Catfish Hunter was nearly as significant for the Yankees as his performance over the final five seasons of his career. An arbitrator found after the 1974 season that Oakland A's owner Charlie Finley had breached Hunter's contract by failing to make an insurance annuity payment. This made Hunter the first major free agent, and though owner George Steinbrenner was serving a suspension for making illegal contributions to Richard Nixon's reelection campaign, his operatives knew his wishes. The Yankees were determined to sign Hunter, even if it took a record contract, and on Dec. 31, 1974, they signed him to a five-year deal worth $3.35 million. Hunter became the highest-paid player in baseball, and the Yankees established themselves as the team other clubs would most fear in free agency. Hunter went 23–14 in his first season with the Yankees, and though he won just 40 games over the next four years, he would help the Yankees win three pennants and two World Series. He won the clincher in 1978 with seven strong innings in Game 6.

REGGIE JACKSON

Of the many free agents George Steinbrenner chased, none paid off with more immediate, overwhelming results than Reggie Jackson. After leading the Oakland A's to three consecutive titles, Jackson migrated to Baltimore in 1976. The next year, Steinbrenner signed him to a five-year, $2.96 million contract, and Jackson earned every penny. He belted three home runs on three consecutive pitches in Game 6 of the 1977 World Series, bringing a title back to the Bronx after 15 years and cementing his reputation as "Mr. October." Steinbrenner often said that his biggest mistake was letting Jackson sign with the Angels after the 1981 World Series, touching off a 14-year playoff dry spell for the Yankees. But Jackson always considered himself a Yankee, working for Steinbrenner as an adviser after his career and choosing a Yankees cap for his plaque in Cooperstown.

DAVE WINFIELD

When George Steinbrenner went free-agent shopping in December 1980, he fell in love with Winfield, a menacing slugger for the San Diego Padres, and envisioned him becoming the next Reggie Jackson. Steinbrenner lavished a 10-year, $23 million contract on Winfield, making him the highest-paid player in the game. But while Winfield won five Gold Gloves and five Silver Slugger awards for the Yankees in the 1980s, he never led them to a championship. He went 1-for-22 in the 1981 World Series, prompting Steinbrenner to dub him "Mr. May," a withering comparison to Jackson. Winfield finally won a title with Toronto in 1992, and when he reached the Hall of Fame in 2001, after compiling 3,110 hits, he chose a Padres cap for his plaque.

Other Yankees Greats

ELSTON HOWARD

Eight years after Jackie Robinson broke the color barrier for the Brooklyn Dodgers, the Yankees finally integrated in 1955 when Elston Howard joined the team. They had signed him from the Kansas City Monarchs of the Negro Leagues in 1950, and Howard developed into a nine-time All-Star, making the team each year from 1957 to 1965. He won the AL MVP award in 1963, two years after batting .348 on the fabled '61 team. A two-time Gold Glove catcher, Howard later helped the Red Sox win the "Impossible Dream" pennant in 1967, a year before his retirement. The Yankees retired Howard's No. 32 in 1984, four years after his death, honoring Howard on his plaque in Monument Park as "a man of great gentleness and dignity."

ROGER MARIS

Like so many others before and since, Roger Maris came to New York as a nondescript player and left with a legacy of greatness. Maris had 58 homers for two teams in the first three years of his career. But in his first two with the Yankees, after the Kansas City A's traded him in December. 1959, Maris slammed 100. The first two came in his Yankees debut, in 1960, the year he captured the MVP award and helped the Yankees recover from a third-place finish to reach the World Series. They won it the next year, after Maris' fierce, but often lonely, battle with Mickey Mantle for the single-season home run record. Maris was worn down by pressure from the media and the feeling that fans did not consider him worthy of eclipsing Babe Ruth's record. But it was Maris—not an injured Mantle—who passed Ruth in the 163rd and final game of the '61 season. His 61 homers in '61 stood as the record for 37 years. Maris would play just five more seasons for the Yankees, but his magic summer lives on in memory.

THURMAN MUNSON

Thurman Munson was the heartbeat of the Yankees in the 1970s, helping the team rise from also-rans to champions. In 1976, the year he won the AL MVP award, Munson was named the Yankees' first captain since Lou Gehrig. A catcher who recognized that his main job was to handle a pitching staff, Munson nonetheless was an offensive force, with a .292 career average and three seasons of 100 RBIs. Intense on the field, Munson had a softer side off it, taking up flying so he could see his family in Ohio on off days. Tragically, he died on Aug. 2, 1979, when the plane he was piloting crashed at the Canton, Ohio, airport, where Munson was practicing takeoffs and landings. The entire Yankees team attended his funeral, and the team has honored Munson by keeping his locker empty ever since. A small "15" hangs above it, forever giving Munson a presence in his clubhouse.

RON GUIDRY

It took more than the signing of Reggie Jackson to make the Yankees champions again in 1977. It took the emergence of Guidry, a 5-foot-11 lefty with just one previous start in the major leagues. Guidry was already 26 in 1977, but he quickly made up for lost time by going 16–7 to help the Yankees win their first World Series in 15 years. In 1978, Guidry etched his name in baseball lore with one of the finest seasons ever for a pitcher. "Louisiana Lightning" used a devastating slider to go 25–3 (the best winning percentage ever for a 20-game winner) and capture the AL Cy Young Award. Guidry struck out 18 Angels on June 17 that season, setting a club record, and won the epic AL East playoff game at Boston. He won 20 games twice in the '80s and also captured five Gold Gloves.

DON MATTINGLY

For years after Mattingly's retirement, no Yankee could inspire warmer cheering. Fans revered him for his feats on the field and his class off it, and he also struck them as a sympathetic figure. The Yankees reached the World Series in 1981, the year before Mattingly's debut. They did not make it back until 1996, just after he retired. The intervening years belonged to Mattingly, the team captain and best player of the mid-1980s. A nine-time Gold Glove winner at first base, Mattingly won the AL batting title in 1984, the MVP in 1985 and set a club record for hits in 1986. It was not quite enough to make the Hall of Fame—back problems robbed him of his power and caused his early retirement—but it was not too bad for a 19th-round draft choice.

BERNIE WILLIAMS

He was gangly and shy, with thick glasses, limited baseball instincts and the uniform number, 51, of a middle reliever. But the young Bernie Williams was earnest and proud and oh, so talented, and he would grow to join the ranks of the great Yankee center fielders. A classical guitarist who quietly strummed by his corner locker at Yankee Stadium, the switch-hitting Williams developed into a Gold Glove winner with speed and power, compiling more hits as a Yankee than anyone besides Gehrig, Ruth and Mantle. His walk-off homers won Game 1 of the ALCS in 1996 and 1999, and he hit above .300 in every season from 1995 through 2002.

PAUL O'NEILL

He seemed to be a known quantity by 1993, an eight-year veteran with a .259 career average, some power and a temper. But Gene Michael, the Yankees' GM, saw more in Paul O'Neill. He believed O'Neill could thrive at Yankee Stadium, where he could pull line drives over the wall and where his talent could blossom away from the Reds' fiery manager, Lou Piniella. Michael swapped Roberto Kelly for O'Neill, and it was the best trade he ever made. O'Neill spearheaded the Yankees' renaissance in the '90s, demanding excellence from himself and others, grinding professional at-bats and winning over fans and George Steinbrenner, who constantly called him "my warrior." A 10-pitch walk in the ninth inning of the 2000 World Series opener sparked a game-tying rally and defined O'Neill's legacy: he was relentless and he played the game right.

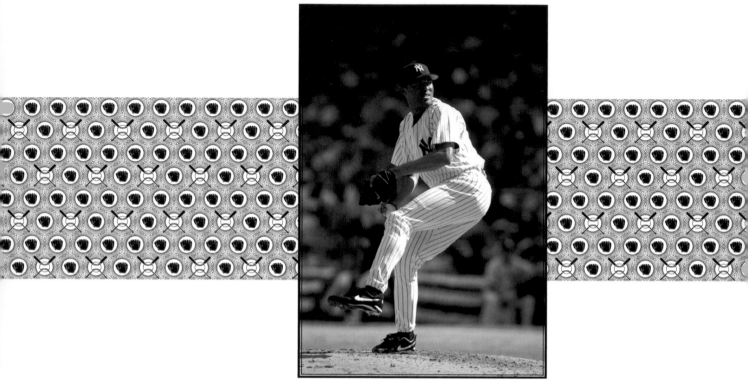

MARIANO RIVERA

As a child on the beaches of Panama, Rivera used cardboard for a glove, a tree branch for a bat
and clothes wrapped in tape for a ball. His father was a fisherman, but Rivera wanted a different
life. He could have been a minister, but his right arm gave him a different destiny. From his
first minor-league season, when he allowed one earned run in 52 innings, Rivera was a Hall of
Famer in waiting. He became the most indispensable Yankee of the Joe Torre era, first as a setup
man in 1996 and then as an overpowering force as a closer. Armed with a devastating cut fastball, Rivera converted 23 consecutive postseason saves, a streak that finally ended in Game 7 of
the 2001 World Series in Arizona. He continued to be one of the dominant relievers in the game
through 2005.

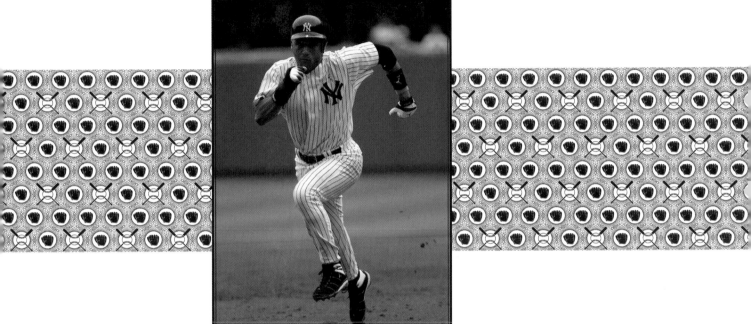

DEREK JETER

Born in New Jersey and raised in Michigan, Jeter would watch the Yankees when they came to Tiger Stadium, snagging outfield seats for a better view of his hero, Dave Winfield. Jeter decided he would grow up to be shortstop for the Yankees. Four years after they drafted him in the first round in 1992, the position was his. Jeter won the Rookie of the Year award in '96, and soon became a worthy successor to Reggie Jackson as a new generation's Mr. October. Whether crashing into the stands for a foul ball in July or swooping for a desperate flip to the plate to save a playoff game, Jeter seemed to lift the Yankees whenever they needed him. No player better understood the demands of George Steinbrenner than Jeter, who believed that a season could not be successful unless it ended with a World Series title. Jeter won four of those in his first five seasons, capping it with the MVP award against the Mets in 2000.

Thurman Munson and teammates celebrate their 1978 World Series victory over the Los Angeles Dodgers.

THE CHAMPIONSHIPS

Since their first World Series title in 1923, the Yankees have collected championships like you or I might collect baseball cards. Here's a rundown of the 26 World Series-winning Yankee ballclubs.

———— New York's World Series Titles ————

1923

The Giants not only beat the Yankees in the World Series in 1921 and 1922, but they also essentially evicted the Yankees from the Polo Grounds. The Yankees responded by building Yankee Stadium and christening it with the first championship in team history. With five 16-game winners on the pitching staff, the Yankees won the pennant by 16 games and faced the Giants again in the World Series. Future Yankee manager Casey Stengel won Game 1 with an inside-the-park homer in the ninth inning, but Babe Ruth, who had hit a career-high .393 in the regular season, belted three homers in a six-game Series victory. The Yankees' status as the little brother of New York baseball was about to change forever.

1927

A second-place finish in 1924 gave way to a lost season in 1925; Babe Ruth's mysterious illness cost him two months, and the Yankees finished in seventh place. In '26, the Yankees lost the last two games of the World Series at home to the Cardinals, and Ruth was caught stealing to end Game 7. But during those wandering seasons, a young first baseman named Lou Gehrig emerged, and in 1927, he and Ruth would lead a club still regarded as the greatest in baseball history. Miller Huggins' team went 110–44, and the lineup would forever be known as "Murderer's Row." Ruth walloped 60 home runs, a record that would stand for 34 years. Gehrig added 47, with 175 RBIs. Ruth, Gehrig, Bob Meusel and Tony Lazzeri all drove in 100 runs, and the pitching staff, led by Waite Hoyt, got a boost from a versatile 30-year-old rookie, Wilcy Moore, who had 19 victories and 13 saves. Moore's complete game clinched a World Series sweep over Pittsburgh, with Ruth, naturally, belting two homers, driving in seven and batting .400 in the four games.

1928

Babe Ruth had hit three homers in a World Series game two years earlier, and he repeated the feat in Game 4 of the '28 Series in St. Louis. Ruth's heroics lifted the Yankees to another sweep, but there were storm clouds ahead. To reach the Series, the Yankees had to hold off the Philadelphia A's, who vaulted into first place on Sept. 8, only to lose a doubleheader before 85,264 fans at Yankee Stadium the next day. That put the Yankees in front for good, but the A's would interrupt their reign atop the American League by winning the next three pennants.

1932

With Joe McCarthy in his second season as the Yankees' manager, no fewer than eight Hall of Famers carried the Yankees to 107 victories, 13 more than Philadelphia. Jimmie Foxx of the A's did wrest the home run crown from the 37-year-old Babe Ruth, who had won it six years in a row, but Ruth made up for it with one of the most memorable long balls in World Series history, his alleged "called shot" in Game 3 at Wrigley Field. The Yankees went on to sweep the Cubs, with Gehrig batting .529 for the series. Gehrig was a remarkable 15-for-28, with seven homers, over the eight games of the 1928 and 1932 World Series.

1936

While Babe Ruth took his place in Cooperstown at the inaugural Hall of Fame induction, a new Yankee legend was born. Joe DiMaggio, 21, broke into a Yankees team still loaded with talent two years after Ruth's last game with the team. DiMaggio batted .323 with 29 homers and 125 RBIs—and did not lead the team in any category. Lou Gehrig (.354-49-152) was still in his prime, and Bill Dickey hit .362, a career high. In the World Series, the Yankees dispatched the Giants in six games. The new kid in center handled the pressure just fine; DiMaggio batted .346 in the Series.

1937

In just his second season, Joe DiMaggio enjoyed his most productive year, batting .346 with 46 homers and 167 runs batted in. With Lou Gehrig and Bill Dickey excelling again, the Yankees paced the American League by 13 games over Detroit. Lefty Gomez and Red Ruffing were the only pitchers in the league with 20 victories. The duo won three times in the five-game World Series victory over the Giants as the Yankees became the first team to win six championships.

1938

Tony Lazzeri's 12-year run at second base had ended after the '37 season, and Joe Gordon replaced him. Gordon, 23, fit seamlessly into the lineup, with 25 homers and 97 RBIs, and he would serve six more distinguished seasons as the Yankees' second baseman. Gordon batted .400 in the Yankees' sweep of the Cubs in the World Series. Nobody knew it at the time, but it would be the last Series for Lou Gehrig, who would be striken with amyotrophic lateral sclerosis the next season and play only eight more games.

1939

The Yankees played the season with a heavy heart. Lou Gehrig, their weakened captain, removed himself from the lineup on May 2. Within a few weeks, the world would know the terrible reason: Gehrig had a rare neuro-muscular disease, A.L.S., and he would never play again. The Yankees would win 106 games, with Babe Dahlgren taking Gehrig's place at first base. Joe DiMaggio won his first MVP award, batting .381, a career high, and leading the Yankees to their fourth title in a row with a World Series sweep of the Cincinnati Reds. Baseball had never seen such a string of excellence as the Yankees displayed in those championship seasons, when they won 16 of 19 games in the World Series.

1941

After a one-year absence, the Yankees rode Joe DiMaggio's 56-game hitting streak to an American League pennant, winning by 17 games over the Red Sox. Back in the World Series, the Yankees kicked off a rivalry with the Brooklyn Dodgers with a five-game victory. The Dodgers set themselves up as heartbroken bridesmaids with a crushing loss in Game 4 at Ebbets Field, when catcher Mickey Owen dropped a third strike with two out and nobody on. Had he caught the ball, the Dodgers would have evened the series, two games apiece. But the low curveball got away from Owen, Tommy Henrich scampered to first to start a winning four-run rally, and the next day the Yankees captured their ninth championship.

1943

With Joe DiMaggio serving in World War II, it was a pitcher, righthander Spud Chandler, who spent a year as the Yankees' brightest star. Chandler went 20–4 with a 1.64 ERA—the lowest in the AL in 24 years—to become the only Yankees pitcher ever to win the MVP award. The Yankees, who were also missing Phil Rizzuto, Red Ruffing and Tommy Henrich, cruised to their third pennant in a row and won a World Series rematch with the Cardinals, who had taken the '42 Series in five games. This time the Yankees took it in five, with Chandler winning twice. He shut out the Cardinals on 10 hits in the finale at Sportsman's Park.

Members of the New York Yankees celebrate a victory over the Boston Red Sox at Fenway Park, Boston, Massachussetts, September 4, 1941.

1947

For the first time in their history, the Yankees won the seventh game of the World Series. They had been to a winner-take-all game just once, when they lost in 1926, and in '47 they must have wondered how the Series got that far. In Game 4, pitcher Bill Bevens was one out away from a no-hitter—albeit with 10 walks—when pinch-hitter Cookie Lavagetto doubled off the right field wall, scoring two runs to give the Dodgers a 3–2 victory. The Yankees won Game 5, and nearly tied Game 6 in the sixth inning when Joe DiMaggio crushed a ball toward the 415-foot mark in left field. A three-run homer would have tied an 8–5 game, but Al Gionfriddo, a defensive replacement, robbed DiMaggio at the fence. DiMaggio kicked the dirt with his spikes—a shocking show of emotion—and the Yankees would go on to lose. But they won that Game 7, falling behind 2–0 but getting 7 $\frac{2}{3}$ shutout relief innings from Bevens and Joe Page to give Manager Bucky Harris his only title with the Yankees.

1949

Joe McCarthy had won seven titles as the Yankees' manager, and with two games left in the 1949 season, a pennant for his new team, the Red Sox, was in his grasp. All the Red Sox had to do was win one of two games at Yankee Stadium. They took a 4–0 lead in the first game but lost, 5–4, as Joe Page shut them down in relief. The next day, Vic Raschi went the distance for his 21st victory, clinching the pennant for new manager Casey Stengel. Back in another World Series against Brooklyn, the Yankees prevailed in five games as Allie Reynolds worked 12 $\frac{1}{3}$ scoreless innings.

1950

The Yankees found a gem in rookie lefthander Whitey Ford. Promoted in June, Ford proceeded to go 9–1 for a staff that included four 15-game winners. Yogi Berra and Joe DiMaggio paced the offense, driving in 246 runs between them, but it was Phil Rizzuto who won the MVP award with his finest season (200 hits, .324 average). The Yankees met the "Whiz Kid" Phillies in the World Series, and after Vic Raschi's 1–0 victory in Game 1, DiMaggio's 10th inning homer off Robin Roberts broke a scoreless tie in Game 2 at Shibe Park. The Yankees won the final two games in the Bronx, sweeping the Series while allowing just five runs.

1951

Once again, the Yankees bid farewell to one superstar and welcomed another. The 19-year-old Mickey Mantle arrived on the scene just as Joe DiMaggio was playing his final season. This was Yogi Berra's turn to be MVP (the first of three in his career), and Allie Reynolds spun two no-hitters. Two other starters, Ed Lopat and Vic Raschi, won 21 games apiece, and the pitching was too much for the Giants in the World Series. After their miracle victory to win the pennant over Brooklyn on Bobby Thomson's "Shot Heard 'Round The World," the Giants struggled for hits against the Yankees. With Lopat and Raschi leading the way, the Yankees had a 1.87 ERA in the Series and won in six games.

1952

With second baseman Jerry Coleman lost to military service for much of the season, the Yankees turned to Billy Martin in hopes of sustaining their dynasty in the post-DiMaggio era. And when Jackie Robinson's bases-loaded pop-up seemed certain to fall in the infield in the seventh inning of Game 7 of the World Series, there was Martin bolting in for a diving catch. The Yankees, who had held off Cleveland by two games to win the pennant, would soon capture their fourth championship in a row. Mickey Mantle batted .311 in his first full season, and capped it with homers in Games 6 and 7 to help the Yankees win the final two games of the Series on the road.

1953

The Yankees won their fifth consecutive World Series, a streak unequalled in baseball history before or since. The legend of Mickey Mantle took flight on the wings of an April 17 homer in Washington that traveled a reported 565 feet (it actually struck a scoreboard 515 feet away). Yogi Berra led the offense again, batting .296 with 27 homers and 108 RBIs. Whitey Ford returned to lead the staff, at 18–6, and the Yankees beat Cleveland easily and met Brooklyn again in the Series. Billy Martin batted .500 (12-for-24), setting a record for hits in a World Series. His final one, a single, drove in Hank Bauer to end Game 6 and clinch the title.

Second baseman Billy Martin rushes in to snag the pop-up off the bat of Jackie Robinson, of the Brooklyn Dodgers, during the seventh inning of Game 7 of the 1952 World Series at Ebbets Field in Brooklyn, New York.

1956

Before the Dodgers headed West after the following season, the Yankees reminded them one last time of who really owned the rivalry. Brooklyn had won its only title at Yankee Stadium in Game 7 of the '55 Series, but the Yankees made history in '56 when Don Larsen authored a perfect game in Game 5. It remains the only postseason no-hitter in major league history, and it gave the Yankees a 3–2 lead in the Series. Though shut out in Game 6, they stormed to a 9–0 victory in Game 7, capping what Mickey Mantle always called his favorite year. Mantle hit .353 with 52 homers and 130 RBIs, taking home the Triple Crown.

1958

Bob Turley became the first AL pitcher to win the Cy Young Award, going 21–7 to help the Yankees win the pennant by 10 games. But Turley's most significant contribution came in the World Series. He could not make it out of the first inning in a blowout loss at Milwaukee in Game 2, and the Yankees lost three of the first four games. In danger of falling to the Braves for the second October in a row, the Yankees turned to Turley. He shut out Milwaukee in Game 5, and when the series shifted back to County Stadium, Turley saved Game 6 and won Game 7 with $6\frac{2}{3}$ innings of relief. It was Casey Stengel's seventh and final championship as the Yankees' manager.

1961

The Yankees had lost a puzzling World Series in 1960, outscoring Pittsburgh by 55–27 but falling in seven games. The loss cost Casey Stengel his job, but Ralph Houk inherited a team that would become one of the most dominant in major league history. With two new teams in the AL and the schedule expanded to 162 games, the Yankees thrived, winning 109 games and an easy pennant. The drama was not found in the standings, but rather on the home run leaderboard. Roger Maris and

Mickey Mantle battled each other for Babe Ruth's home run record, with Maris pulling his 61st homer on the final day of the season off Boston's Tracy Stallard. Injured at the end of the season, Mantle finished with 54. The World Series against the Reds was anticlimactic; the Yankees won in five, boosted by 14 shutout innings by Whitey Ford. An exhausted Maris hit .105 for the Series, but one of his two hits was a homer to win Game 3 at Crosley Field.

Versus the San Francisco Giants, 1962

1962

Ralph Terry had given up the home run to Bill Mazeroski that ended the 1960 World Series. Two years later, he tossed a shutout in the Series finale — but the final pitch he threw was similarly hard hit. The San Francisco Giants' Willie McCovey lined out to second baseman Bobby Richardson with runners on second and third and two outs in the bottom of the ninth, preserving a 1–0 Yankees victory and the team's 10th title since the end of World War II. Charlie Brown, of all people, summed up the sentiment for Giants fans. "Peanuts" author Charles Schultz, a Giants fan, drew a strip in which Charlie Brown and Linus sat silently for three panels. Finally, Charlie Brown loses it, blurting out, "Why couldn't McCovey have hit the ball three feet higher?" The Yankees had done it again, and they would reach the Series again the next two years. Little did they know it then, but this championship would be their last for 15 years.

1977

George Steinbrenner bought a moribund Yankees franchise in 1973, and three years later, the team was in the World Series. That achievement, Steinbrenner has said, was his proudest moment as a Yankee, but the Series itself brought disappointment: the Reds swept the Yankees in four. Steinbrenner reloaded in the off-season, signing Reggie Jackson and pitcher Don Gullett as free agents, and Billy Martin's Yankees won another pennant, coming back in the deciding ALCS game to beat the Royals on the road. Jackson clashed with Martin all year—the two nearly brawled in the Fenway Park dugout on June 18—but he capped a 32-homer, 110-RBI season with a breathtaking performance in the World Series. With three swings in the Game 6 clincher against the Dodgers at Yankee Stadium, Jackson restored the majesty of the Yankees. It was the first three-homer game in the World Series since Babe Ruth in 1928, and the Yankees were the champions.

1978

Proving that he would never be satisfied, George Steinbrenner signed free agent closer Goose Gossage before the '78 season—even though his current closer, Sparky Lyle, had won the Cy Young Award in '77. Gossage would be the man on the mound for the last outs of the regular season, the ALCS and the World Series, but the road there was treacherous. On July 19, the Yankees sat in fourth place in the East, 14 games behind the Red Sox. Within a week, Billy Martin would be fired and replaced with Bob Lemon, who guided the Yankees on an historic surge as Ron Guidry went 25–3 to win the Cy Young Award. The

Yankees clobbered the Red Sox in a four-game sweep at Fenway Park in September dubbed the "Boston Massacre" (combined score: 42–9), and took the one-game playoff on Oct. 2, 5–4, on the strength of a three-run homer by Bucky Dent and a solo shot by Reggie Jackson. The Yankees then knocked out Kansas City in four, lost the first two games of the World Series in Los Angeles and won the last four in succession to repeat as champions. Catfish Hunter clinched the title by winning Game 6 in his final postseason appearance, and Dent led the Yankees with 10 hits to win the Series MVP.

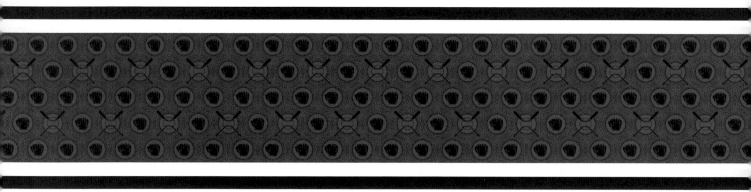

1996

Don Mattingly had retired after the '95 division series, when the Mariners shocked the Yankees at the raucous Kingdome. Manager Buck Showalter resigned, Joe Torre took over to little fanfare, Tino Martinez replaced Mattingly and Derek Jeter broke in at shortstop. All the moves worked to perfection. With homegrown stars like Jeter, Andy Pettitte, Bernie Williams and Mariano Rivera bolstering the veteran core of David Cone, Jimmy Key, John Wetteland and Paul O'Neill, the Yankees stormed into their first World Series since 1981, helped by a 12-year-old fan, Jeffrey Maier, who deflected Jeter's fly ball into the stands for a homer in

Game 1 of the ALCS against Baltimore. In the World Series, the defending champion Braves humbled the Yankees in the Bronx, winning the first two games by a combined score of 16–1. But Cone won Game 3 in Atlanta, Jim Leyritz slugged a pivotal three-run homer the next night, and Andy Pettitte beat John Smoltz, 1–0, in Game 5. The Yankees came home to beat Greg Maddux in Game 6, with Charlie Hayes squeezing the final foul out and Wetteland leaping into Joe Girardi's arms. After 18 years, the Yankees were kings of the hill, top of the heap, A-Number-One again.

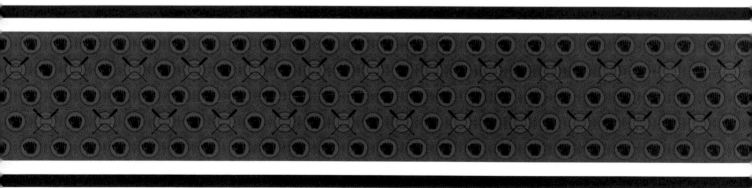

1998

After an upset loss to Cleveland in the 1997 division series, the Yankees started '98 with three successive losses on the West Coast. Little did they know that they would soon become the greatest Yankees team since the fabled 1927 champions. The Yankees went 114–48 in the regular season, with a .704 winning percentage that ranked just shy of the 1927 club record (.714). Bernie Williams won the batting title with a .339 average, Orlando Hernandez gave the rotation a jolt, and newcomers Scott Brosius and Chuck Knoblauch fit snugly into the lineup. After coming back from a 2–1 deficit to beat Cleveland in the ALCS, the Yankees swept the Padres in the World Series, with MVP Brosius slugging a pivotal Game 3 homer off Trevor Hoffman. Including the postseason, the '98 Yankees had a sparkling overall record of 125–50 and cemented their place among the great teams of all time.

1999

A trying season culminated in the most dominant postseason run of the Joe Torre era. The Yankees mourned the death of Joe DiMaggio that March, and Torre battled prostate cancer in spring training, missing the first 36 games of the season. Roger Clemens, acquired from Toronto for David Wells and two others, struggled through an inconsistent season as he adjusted to New York. But Derek Jeter had his best season, batting .349, and in October, the Yankees picked up where they had left off in San Diego the previous fall. They won 11 of 12 games in the postseason, culminating in a World Series sweep of Atlanta.

2000

The Yankees won just 87 games in the regular season, the fewest of any pinstriped title team. But after dropping 15 of their final 18 games down the stretch, they rallied in October to face the Mets in the first subway series since 1956. Each game was decided by one or two runs, and the Yankees prevailed with more October magic. Derek Jeter won the World Series MVP award, and mid-season acquisition David Justice added thump to the middle of the lineup. Bernie Williams caught Mike Piazza's fly ball in deep center field to end the Series, kneeling on the grass at Shea Stadium as the celebration began.

Victory over the Mets, 2000

YANKEES SUPERLATIVES

Whittling down the greatest moments and individual performances in the storied history of the Yankees is a nearly impossible task, but some highlights leap to mind when assessing the franchise's remarkable history.

—————— The Greatest Moments ——————

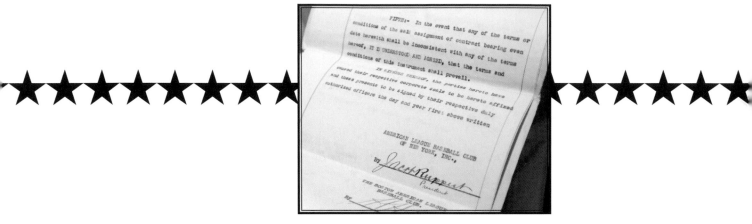

THE YANKEES PURCHASE THE BABE

On July 29, 1919, the Boston Red Sox sold ace pitcher Carl Mays, who had won the deciding game of the previous year's World Series, to the Yankees for $40,000 and two players. Harry Frazee, the Red Sox owner, discovered then that the Yankees were an easy source of cash. So when Babe Ruth demanded a raise after swatting 29 homers in 1919 to set the single-season home run record, Frazee knew where to look. He brokered a sale to the Yankees that would more than double the previous record ever paid for a player. It did not matter to Frazee that the Yankees had eclipsed his team in the standings, winning 20 more games than they had in 1918 while the

Red Sox tumbled from world champs to sixth place. Frazee had a chance to make $125,000 in cash for Ruth—plus a $350,000 loan against the mortgage on Fenway Park—and on Jan. 3, 1920, he took it. Frazee was a New Yorker who produced Broadway plays, though the infamous "No, No, Nanette," which is often cited as the reason he needed cash in 1920, did not debut until 1923. In any event, Frazee's pledge to use the money to buy other players never materialized, and the sale sentenced the Red Sox to 86 years without a championship. Almost instantly, it elevated the Yankees to the status of the premier team in sports.

THE CALLED SHOT

Babe Ruth had a lot of reasons to be riled up at the Chicago Cubs and their fans on Oct. 1, 1932. Ruth's buddy and ex-teammate, Mark Koenig, had helped the Cubs reach the World Series but had been voted just a half-share of their prize money. Some 50,000 fans in tiny Wrigley Field were also heckling Ruth, throwing lemons at him; one fan even spat on Ruth's wife that day. The Cubs' players were needling him incessantly. "Every time I went to bat," Ruth said, as quoted by author Harvey Frommer, "the Cubs on the bench would yell, 'Oogly googly.'" Ruth responded with a homer early in Game 3, and Charley Root got two called strikes on him in the fifth. After the second one, Ruth said, Cubs catcher Gabby Hartnett razzed him with another "oogly googly." At that point, Ruth would always maintain, he barked at the Cubs bench that he would "knock this one a mile," and pointed to the right field bleachers. That is where he clobbered the ball for his 15th and final World Series homer. Root claimed that if Ruth had truly pointed to the bleachers, he would have hit him with a pitch. A widely held theory is that Ruth was simply motioning to the Cubs' bench on the third-base side, reminding them that he still had one strike left. There was no consensus among the many eyewitnesses, but that hardly seems to matter. The idea that the story is even remotely plausible is a testament to Ruth's cocksure spirit and legendary power.

DON LARSEN'S PERFECT GAME

When he struck out Dale Mitchell on a check swing for the last out of the finest pitching performance in World Series history, Don Larsen simply trotted back toward the home dugout at Yankee Stadium. His catcher, Yogi Berra, was having nothing of it. This 2–0 victory over Brooklyn in Game 5 of the 1956 World Series, this perfect game, was a cause for celebration. "In self-defense, Larsen caught Berra in mid-air as one would catch a frolicking child," Shirley Povich wrote in the *Washington Post*, "and that's how they made their way toward the Yankee bench, Larsen carrying Berra." The iconic image has stuck all these years later, as no pitcher has thrown another

no-hitter in the postseason. Larsen—who, two years before, had gone 3–21 for the Baltimore Orioles—threw 97 pitches in his gem, running a three-ball count just once, in the first inning. The only close call came on a second-inning smash by Jackie Robinson that deflected off third baseman Andy Carey's glove. The shortstop, Gil McDougald, grabbed it on a hop and threw out Robinson at first. Larsen would strike out seven Dodgers, ending with Mitchell, who was batting for pitcher Sal Maglie. Mickey Mantle's fourth-inning homer supplied all the offense Larsen needed, and the Yankees won the World Series two games later.

CHRIS CHAMBLISS' HOME RUN

Six outs from clinching their first pennant since 1964, the Yankees lost a 6–3 lead in Game 5 of the 1976 ALCS when Kansas City's George Brett ripped a three-run homer to tie the game. But that only served to heighten the drama. With the score tied, 6–6, Chris Chambliss led off the bottom of the ninth inning by slamming Mark Littell's first pitch to deep right field, sending the ball into the dark Bronx night. The Yankees won the pennant and the crowd went berserk. It seemed as if all 56,821 fans stormed the field at once, mobbing Chambliss as he pushed and shoved his way around the bases. He escaped to the dugout before even trying to tag the plate, but the Royals did not object. The fans had caused some $100,000 in damage, but the Yankees were back in the World Series. Chambliss never hit more than 20 homers in a season, but this one was unforgettable.

REGGIE'S 3-HOMER GAME

There were 56,407 fans at Yankee Stadium on Oct. 18, 1977, for Game 6 of the World Series. Yet Steve Garvey, the Dodgers' first baseman, was quite sure he could get away with cheering Reggie Jackson in full view of the crowd. "When I was sure nobody was looking," Garvey said, "I applauded in my glove." Even opponents had to admit it: Jackson morphed from superstar to immortal with his third home run of the game. He had homered in his last at-bat of Game 5, in Los Angeles, and then walked in his first plate appearance of Game 6. Three swings later, Jackson had put his signature on baseball history. He slammed three first-pitch home runs—off Burt Hooten in the fourth inning, Elias Sosa in the fifth and Charlie Hough in the eighth—to give him a record five for the World Series. The last shot landed in the faraway black seats at the remodeled Yankee Stadium. Only Babe Ruth had hit three homers in a World Series game before Jackson, who won his fourth championship ring.

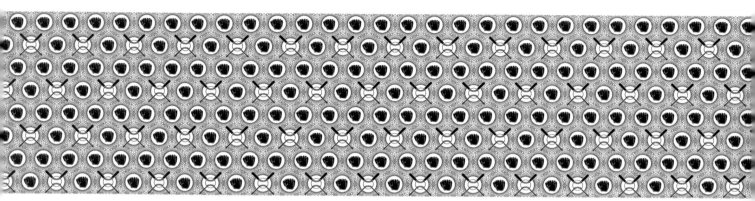

BUCKY DENT

The simple call by Bill White still gives a Yankee fan chills. "Deep to left," White said on Oct. 2, 1978, his voice rising, hoping. "Yastrzemski"—pause—"will not get it, it's a home run! A three-run homer by Bucky Dent, and the Yankees now lead by a score of 3–2!" The homer, through the afternoon shadows, was crushing to the Red Sox (Carl Yastrzemski buckled when it cleared the Green Monster) and inspiring to the Yankees. Dent had homered just four times that season and was using Mickey Rivers' bat. The pitch before, Dent had fouled a ball off his foot, causing a delay while trainer Gene Monahan tended to him.

Mike Torrez, who had been on the mound for the last out of the Yankees' World Series title in 1977, said he should have taken warm-ups to stay loose. Instead, Torrez left his next pitch, a fastball, too far inside. Dent yanked it down the line and into history. The blast did not end the game—a double by Thurman Munson and a homer by Reggie Jackson would follow—but the Yankees never trailed after Dent's seventh-inning shot. They would win the division when Yastrzemski popped out to Graig Nettles with runners at the corners with two out in the bottom of the ninth.

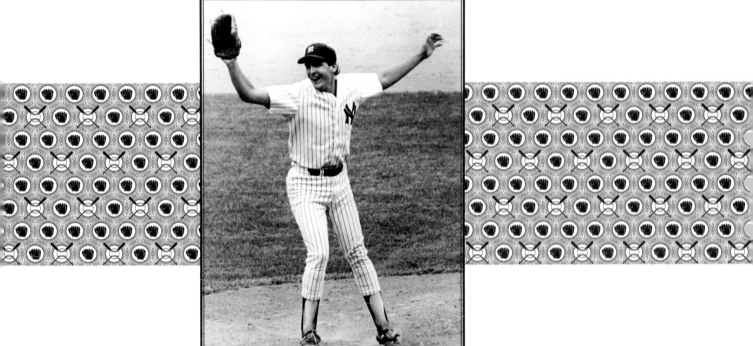

A HAPPY 4TH

Wade Boggs was a scientist of hitting, honing a sweet swing that produced 3,010 career hits. But on July 4, 1983, playing for the Boston Red Sox, Boggs took possibly the weakest swing of his career. Dave Righetti was the reason. With two outs and two strikes in the ninth inning, Righetti badly fooled Boggs on a slider, whiffing that year's A.L. batting champ and completing the first no-hitter by a Yankee since Don Larsen's perfect game in the 1956 World Series. Righetti walked four and struck out nine, including seven in the first three innings. Banished to the minors a year earlier by the impatient principal owner, George Steinbrenner, Righetti picked the perfect date to twirl a no-hitter: July 4 is Steinbrenner's birthday. The fact that it came against the hated Red Sox was gravy.

David Wells

DAVID WELLS' PERFECT GAME

It was Beanie Baby Day at Yankee Stadium, a Sunday afternoon in May 1998, and thousands of kids had no idea they would get a lifelong memory along with their free stuffed bear. But David Wells, the burly, bawdy lefthander, made history. After waking up with a raging hangover from partying too hard the night before, Wells chugged coffee in the clubhouse and then silenced the Minnesota Twins on the field. He struck out 11 in a 4-0 victory, riding off the field on his teammates' shoulders after Paul O'Neill caught Pat Meares' fly ball to end the game. Wells became the first Yankee to throw a perfect game since Don Larsen—a fellow graduate of Point Loma High School in San Diego.

DAVID CONE'S PERFECT GAME

A year and two months after David Wells' date with perfection, Cone had his own. Don Larsen, of all people, threw out the first pitch that Sunday, before the Yankees played the Montreal Expos in an interleague game. None of the Expos had ever faced Cone before, and he baffled them with his fastballs and, especially, his Frisbee slider. Cone whiffed 10 of the young Expos, falling to his knees, overcome with emotion, as Scott Brosius caught Orlando Cabrera's foul pop to end the game. Cone was 36 at the time, and this would be his last great season. He slipped to 4-14 in 2000, and he would never throw another complete game or shutout again.

TINO AND BROSIUS GO DEEP

Deep down, Tino Martinez knew the Yankees would replace him after the 2001 season. And Scott Brosius, who played across the diamond from Martinez at third base, knew he would retire at year's end. But both players had one last moment within them. On consecutive nights in the 2001 World Series, Martinez and Brosius crunched game-tying homers in the ninth inning off Arizona submariner Byung-Hyun Kim. Martinez did it in Game 4, setting up Derek Jeter's game-winning homer in the 10th. Incredibly, Brosius pulled off the same feat the next night, and the Yankees won in 12 innings to take a 3–2 series lead. They would lose Games 6 and 7 in Arizona, but for many fans in a city reeling from the Sept. 11 terrorist attacks, the last two home games of that season would always have special resonance.

Tino Martinez and Paul O'Neill celebrate after Martinez's two-run ninth-inning home run during Game 4 of the 2001 World Series.

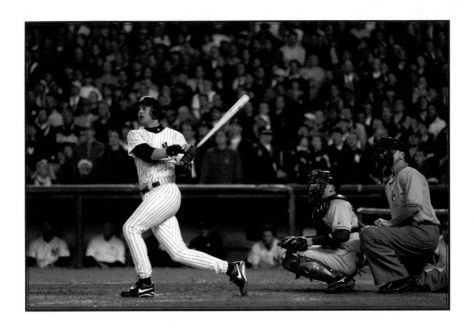

AARON BLEEPIN' BOONE

By Game 7 of the 2003 ALCS, against the Boston Red Sox, Aaron Boone had earned a spot on the Yankees' bench with a .194 average in the postseason. As the Yankees roared back from a 5–2 deficit to tie the game against a fading Pedro Martinez—what was Boston manager Grady Little thinking!—Boone could only watch. But Willie Randolph, the third-base coach, had a premonition that Boone would make an impact after entering the game as a pinch-runner. Randolph told Boone he would do something big, and Boone came through with a walk-off homer on Tim Wakefield's first pitch in the bottom of the 11th inning. As the ball soared into the left field seats, Boone spread his arms wide and glided around the bases. Babe Ruth's curse would live for another year, and the Yankees had won the pennant.

Great Individual Performances

THE BABE'S 54, 59 AND 60-HOMER SEASONS

Frank Baker, a Hall of Fame third baseman for the A's and the Yankees, was such a prolific power hitter that his nickname was "Home Run." In 1919, Baker hit 11 for the Yankees to finish second in the American League. The leader, Babe Ruth of the Boston Red Sox, hit 29—an unprecedented power explosion. The previous holder of the single-season record, Ned Williamson of the Chicago White Stockings, had hit 27 in a small ballpark in 1884. Now Ruth had the record, and he would break his mark three times. In 1920, his first season with the Yankees, Ruth belted 54 home runs (the runner-up hit 19), and his slugging percentage, .847, would stand as the single-season record until Barry Bonds broke it in 2001. But Ruth was not done there. In 1921,

he walloped 59 homers, 35 more than the runner-up. He was more than doubling his closest competition, and at 26 years old, Ruth was already the career home run leader, passing Roger Connor's mark of 138. But his most memorable feat came in 1927. Only about 10,000 fans showed up for the game against Washington on Sept. 30, when Ruth slugged his 60th home run off Tom Zachary. It was a standard that wouldn't be topped until 1961, when the schedule was expanded from 154 games to 162. Though the fans hardly packed Yankee Stadium to see it, sportswriters sensed the majesty of what Ruth had done. Wrote Paul Gallico: "Succumb to the power and romance of the man."

GEHRIG'S STREAK

On May 6, 1925, the Yankees released short-stop Everett Scott, who had played in a record 1,307 consecutive games. A weak hitter named Pee Wee Wanninger replaced Scott, and Lou Gehrig pinch-hit for Wanninger in a game on June 1. Thus began Gehrig's streak of 2,130 games, which would easily eclipse Scott's mark and would last until Cal Ripken broke it in 1995. Gehrig was just 21 years old, two years out of Columbia University, and not yet established as an everyday player when Miller Huggins inserted him into the starting lineup for veteran Wally Pipp on June 2. The popular story is that Pipp had a headache from a batting-practice beaning and asked for a day off. Other sources claim the beaning occurred a month later, and Huggins was simply trying to shake up a struggling lineup. In any case, Gehrig quickly established himself, and Pipp was sold to the Reds the next year. Gehrig finally took himself out of the lineup in Detroit on May 2, 1939, giving in to the disease that would claim his life two years later.

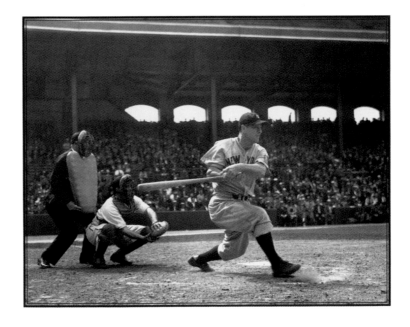

DiMaggio's 56-game hitting streak

When Joe DiMaggio hit in 56 games in a row in 1941, it was not even the longest streak of his professional career. In 1933, when he was just 18 years old, DiMaggio hit in 61 straight for the San Francisco Seals of the Pacific Coast League. Destined for stardom, DiMaggio had four championships and two batting titles to his name by '41. His famous streak, which may be the most venerable record in baseball, began on May 15 when he went 1-for-4 against the White Sox. It continued for more than two months through eight cities and the All-Star break, and included hits off four future Hall of Famers. The streak captivated the nation until its end on July 17 in Cleveland, when Indians third baseman Ken Keltner robbed DiMaggio twice with back-handed stabs. DiMaggio, who batted .408 during the streak (91 for 223), promptly started a 16-game streak the next game. His heroics inspired a song by the Les Brown Band, which included this unforgettable reminder: "He's just a man and not a freak—Joltin' Joe DiMaggio."

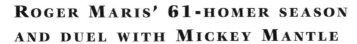

ROGER MARIS' 61-HOMER SEASON AND DUEL WITH MICKEY MANTLE

Roger Maris died in 1985, at 51 years old, too soon to see the bulky sluggers of a later generation shatter his treasured home run record. But its importance to Maris is written on his gravestone in Fargo, N.D. The engraving tells the story of Maris' improbable achievement: "Against All Odds," it says, under an image of Maris' swing with the numbers "61, '61." Maris truly did overcome the odds to topple Babe Ruth's 34-year-old record of 60 home runs in a season. He was not the Yankee favored to do it; Mickey Mantle was. He had no history of explosive power, beyond the 39 homers he had hit in 1960. And as a private person, he did not seem cut out for the scrutiny and the hype around his chase; his hair fell out due to stress that summer. But Maris broke the record, coming through on the final day of the season—in game 163, a longer schedule than in 1927—by driving a pitch from Boston's Tracy Stallard into the right field seats at Yankee Stadium. Injuries had curtailed Mantle's chase at 54, leaving Maris with a singular achievement that no asterisk—real or imagined—could diminish.

RON GUIDRY'S 1978 SEASON

For the Yankees, 1978 will always be remembered for the most stirring comeback in franchise history, a recovery from a 14-game hole to catch the Boston Red Sox and win the AL East. But not all the Yankees slumbered through the first half. Ron Guidry started 13–0, and he maintained his excellence right through Game 163, when he beat the Red Sox in the one-game playoff to run his record to an astonishing 25–3. The season was a bolt of Louisiana Lightning, coming in just Guidry's second full year in the majors. Guidry had a 1.74 ERA, nine shutouts and 248 strikeouts, including 18 in one game against the Angels on June 17. Fans stood and cheered whenever Guidry got to two strikes that night, starting a tradition that has lived on. The only way to beat Guidry in '78, it seemed, was to start a pitcher named Mike: his losses came against Mike Caldwell, Mike Flanagan and Mike Willis. Then again, the pitcher Guidry beat in the one-game playoff was Mike Torrez.

Joe Torre

YANKEES SKIPPERS

New York has been led by an eclectic mix of motivators, tacticians and out-and-out geniuses. Five names stand above the rest.

MILLER HUGGINS

Miller Huggins fashioned a 13-year major league career out of precious little talent. Just 5-foot-6 and 140 pounds, "Mighty Mite" scrapped his way to a regular second base job with the Reds and Cardinals by studying the game, drawing more than 1,000 walks and bringing his attention to detail to his job as manager, first with the Cardinals while he was still playing, and then, in 1918, to the Yankees. Huggins' keen scouting eye helped form the Yankees' early dynasty, and he often quizzed his players on the bench about game situations. Waite Hoyt, the Hall of Fame pitcher, called him a "schoolmaster in the dugout." Huggins stayed there until his death in 1929, winning the Yankees' first three championships. The first monument at Yankee Stadium was in his honor, lauding Huggins' "splendid character" and "priceless contributions to baseball."

JOE MCCARTHY

Joe McCarthy had taken the Cubs to the World Series in 1929, but when he joined the Yankees in 1931, there was some sentiment that Babe Ruth should have been named manager. Ruth never realized that dream, but he kept quiet as McCarthy took over. A disciplinarian who forbade card-playing in the clubhouse, McCarthy was expected to produce. Ed Barrow, the Yankees' Hall of Fame chief executive, told McCarthy that the club owner, Colonel Jacob Ruppert, expected a pennant by year two. McCarthy delivered, winning the World Series in 1932 and again from 1936 through 1939. A pioneer in the use of pitchers—assigning specific roles as starters and relievers—McCarthy would capture seven championships in all, tied with Casey Stengel for the most of any manager in history.

CASEY STENGEL

Like Joe Torre many years later, Casey Stengel came to the Yankees after an uneventful managing career in other places. Stengel had guided the Dodgers and the Braves for nine seasons, never finishing higher than fifth place. But in 12 seasons in pinstripes, Stengel won 10 pennants and seven World Series titles. Sportswriters delighted in covering Stengel, who entertained them with his uniquely fractured logic, such as, "Good pitching will always stop good hitting—and vice versa." But the man they called "The Old Perfessor" knew what he was doing in the dugout. He platooned players to great effect when few other managers were doing it. By getting the most from his strong bench, Stengel kept slumping players from doing much damage. His many stars— Joe DiMaggio, Yogi Berra, Mickey Mantle, Whitey Ford—did the rest.

BILLY MARTIN

George Steinbrenner was addicted to Billy Martin, hiring and firing him five times from 1975 to 1988. Martin had already worn out his welcome in Minnesota, Detroit and Texas, and Steinbrenner knew he was getting more than a savvy baseball man. "The game is important," Steinbrenner said, "but so is the showmanship involved with the game." So it was with Martin, who feuded in public with his owner and his star players, notably Reggie Jackson. Sometimes, his pushing and prodding worked: the Yankees reached the World Series in 1976 under Martin and won it the next year. But Martin did not last through '78, and subsequent trials in '79, '83, '85 and '88 produced no more playoff appearances. Still, Martin had a .591 winning percentage as Yankees' manager, and if he had not died in a car crash on Christmas Day 1989 at age 61, there is a strong chance Steinbrenner would have hired him again.

JOE TORRE

If it seems as if the pressure never gets to Joe Torre, it's not an act. Real pressure, Torre knows from experience, comes from managing a team low on talent. Torre experienced plenty of that before arriving in the Bronx after the 1995 season. He had managed for 14 seasons with the Mets, Braves and Cardinals, never reaching the World Series. But with the Yankees, Torre was the right man at the right time. With trusted coaches Don Zimmer and Mel Stottlemyre, who had starred on the mound for the Yankees from 1964 to 1974, Torre maintained a calm exterior and used extraordinary communication skills to stabilize the clubhouse. Had the team not captured four World Series titles in Torre's first five years, Steinbrenner might have been inclined to dump Torre, the way he had discarded so many managers in the past. But when tension reached a boiling point in their relationship, Steinbrenner always softened, understanding that, while his money had helped Torre rise to Hall of Fame status, Torre was more popular and better at his job than any manager he had ever had.

TALKIN' YANKEES BASEBALL

"I'd like to thank the good Lord for making me a Yankee." JOE DiMAGGIO, AS QUOTED BELOW THE MARQUEE AT YANKEE STADIUM

"Fans, for the past two weeks you have been reading about the bad break I got. Yet today, I consider myself the luckiest man on the face of the earth. I have been in ballparks for 17 years and have never received anything but kindness and encouragement from you fans." LOU GEHRIG, JULY 4, 1939, FAREWELL ADDRESS

"I'd play for half my salary if I could hit in this dump all my life." BABE RUTH, AFTER SLAMMING NINE BATTING-PRACTICE HOME RUNS AT WRIGLEY FIELD BEFORE GAME 3 OF THE 1932 WORLD SERIES, WHEN HE HIT THE FAMOUS "CALLED SHOT" HOMER

"Talking to Yogi Berra about baseball is like talking to Homer about the gods." A. BARTLETT GIAMATTI, FORMER COMMISSIONER OF BASEBALL

Yogi-isms

"It ain't over til it's over." ... *"When you come to a fork in the road, take it."* ... *"Baseball is 90 percent mental. The other half is physical."* ... *"This is like déjà vu all over again."* ... *"The future ain't what it used to be."* ... *"If the fans don't want to come out to the ballpark, no one can stop 'em."* ... *"You can observe a lot just by watching."* ... *"I never said most of the things I said."*

"My goals are to hit .300, score 100 runs and stay injury-prone." MICKEY RIVERS

"To think you're a .300 hitter and end up at .237 in your last season, then find yourself looking at a lifetime .298 average—it made me want to cry." MICKEY MANTLE

"Somebody once asked me if I ever went up to the plate trying to hit a home run. I said, 'Sure, every time.'" MICKEY MANTLE

"It was all I lived for, to play baseball." MICKEY MANTLE

"The Yankees don't pay me to win every day—just two out of three." CASEY STENGEL

"I became a Hall of Famer here. When (Dan) Duquette said that I was done, if I'd have taken his advice and went home, I wouldn't have been a Hall of Famer. So it's a no-brainer. It's definitely pretty easy. Reggie spent five years here, and this will be five for me."* ROGER CLEMENS IN 2003, EXPLAINING WHY HE WANTS TO ENTER THE HALL OF FAME AS A YANKEE

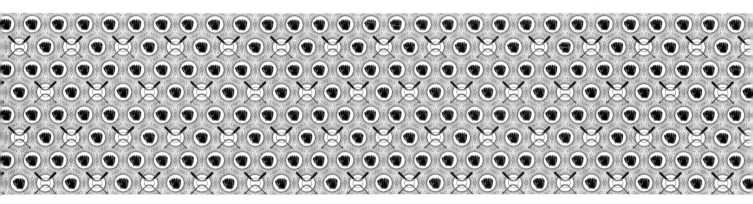

"I won't be active in the day-to-day operations of the club at all." GEORGE STEINBRENNER, UPON BUYING THE YANKEES IN 1973

"Where have you gone, Joe DiMaggio? A nation turns its lonely eyes to you." PAUL SIMON, 1968

"Where is it written that if you don't get results right away, you fire people? What kind of asinine policy is that?" GEORGE STEINBRENNER, MOCKING HIMSELF IN A SKIT ON *SATURDAY NIGHT LIVE* IN 1990

"One's a born liar, the other's convicted." BILLY MARTIN'S FAMOUS PUTDOWN OF REGGIE JACKSON AND GEORGE STEINBRENNER

"I'm the straw that stirs the drink. Munson thinks he can be the straw that stirs the drink, but he can only stir it bad." REGGIE JACKSON, WHO CLAIMED HE WAS MISQUOTED, IN *SPORT MAGAZINE* IN 1977

Catfish Hunter and Reggie Jackson

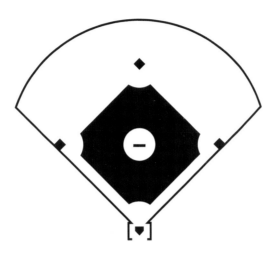

"To me, he's the greatest modern-day weapon I have seen or played against.

He has been the heart and soul of the New York Yankees dynasty."

ALEX RODRIGUEZ ON MARIANO RIVERA

This Page: *Steve Garvey of the Dodgers is tagged at the plate by Thurman Munson during the 1977 World Series.*

Facing Page: *Yankees GM Ed Barrow sits in the Ebbets Field stands with Dodgers GM Branch Rickey prior to a World Series game in 1952.*

THE RIVALRIES

The Yankees have built their legend in large part on their rivalries with two other storied clubs. In fact, some of the greatest moments in Yankee history have come at the expense of the Dodgers and Red Sox.

Dodgers

From 1903 through 1957, there were three major league teams in New York. The last to arrive was the Yankees, who spent their first two years in Baltimore and then became the New York Highlanders. The Yankees shared ballparks with the Giants in the early years, and the teams faced off in the World Series five times in the 1920s and '30s.

To the Yankees, the other New York team was an afterthought. Dodgers? Robins? Superbas? Whatever they were called, they were not a threat to the Yankees. After buying

Gene Woodling of the Yankees slides into home plate past catcher Roy Campanella, of the Brooklyn Dodgers, during the 1949 World Series.

Babe Ruth from the Red Sox in 1920, the Yankees played in 11 World Series over the next two decades. In none of those seasons did the Brooklyn team finish higher than third.

In fact, as Yogi Berra once wrote, if the Yankees had to play in a subway series, they preferred the Giants because more fans could pack the Polo Grounds than Ebbets Field, raising the gate receipts and boosting the winners' bonus checks.

Alas, the Yankees would soon see plenty of the Dodgers. As the Giants faded following their World Series losses to the Yankees in '36 and '37, the Dodgers crept up in the NL standings. Under player-manager Leo Durocher, they rose from third to second to 100 victories in 1941 and their first pennant in 21 years.

It was a memorable team, with first baseman Dolph Camilli enjoying a career year (34 homers at age 34) and 22-year-old Pete Reiser taking the batting title, at .343. Another 22-year-old, shortstop Pee Wee Reese, became a full-time starter that season, a position he would hold for the rest of the franchise's lifespan in Brooklyn.

The Yankees, meanwhile, rode Joe DiMaggio's 56-game hitting streak to their fifth World Series in six years. It set up the first of

11 Series confrontations with the Dodgers, and this one set the pattern.

The Yankees broke ahead, two games to one, and the Dodgers led by a run in the ninth inning of Game 4. The first three Yankees batters made outs. So how did the Dodgers not win and tie the series? Catcher Mickey Owen dropped the third strike to the third hitter, Tommy Henrich, who reached first on the error. The Yankees went on to score four runs and win the game, 7–4. They won the Series the next day.

Elation in the Bronx. Heartbreak in Brooklyn. It seemed to be the fates of the franchises. The stereotypes fixed the images. The Yankees were the cool, corporate superpower. The Dodgers were the colorful, plucky underdogs. The Yankees won—a job well done. The Dodgers lost—wait 'til next year.

For the players, the rivalry was mostly friendly. The teams would meet a few times in spring training—Yankees pitchers habitually dusted off Roy Campanella for fun—but never faced each other often enough to develop real enmity.

After the '41 Series, the Cardinals rose in the National League, winning four of the next five pennants. But in '47, the historic season in which Jackie Robinson broke the color barrier, the Dodgers returned by beating St. Louis for the pennant by five games. The Yankees, naturally, were waiting for them.

The Dodgers scored the most memorable victory of the Series, spoiling Bill Bevens' no-hit bid with two outs in the ninth inning of Game 4, turning the Yankees from winners to losers on the final swing of the game by Cookie Lavagetto, who doubled in two runs. But the Yankees would win two of the next three games to take the series.

By '49, the Dodgers seemed poised to finally knock off the Yankees. Robinson was the National League's MVP, while first baseman Gil Hodges, right fielder Duke Snider and catcher Campanella had established themselves as productive everyday players. But the World Series was no contest—Yanks in five, including the final three games at Ebbets Field.

The Dodgers got a little closer in '52 and '53, pushing the Yankees to Game 7 the first year and Game 6 the next. But both times the Yankees prevailed, and "Dem Bums," the Dodgers' affectionate nickname, ran their losing streak against the Yankees to five World Series.

Even the glory of 1955 was short-lived. The Dodgers finally triumphed over the Yankees, with Johnny Podres, a 23-year-old lefty, spinning a 2–0 shutout in Game 7 at Yankee Stadium. Sandy Amoros, a defensive replacement in left field, robbed Yogi Berra of an extra-base hit that could have tied the game in the sixth inning, tracking down his fly ball at the wall in left, fully extended with his right glove hand.

Church bells clanged out across Brooklyn after Elston Howard grounded to Reese for the final out. The wait was over, but the Yankees took the Series in '56, highlighted by Don Larsen's perfect game in Game 5. After the next season, the Dodgers moved to Los Angeles.

It was a crippling blow to a fan base that had cheered for the Dodgers with a childlike enthusiasm, as part of the neighborhood, the boys in blue down the block. Now, the Dodgers played 3,000 miles away, gone forever. The rivalry with the Yankees, at least, remained.

The reason was simple: for years, the teams would shadow each other from across the leagues. When the Yankees were good, generally, so were the Dodgers. They still had to put aside the Giants now and then—in New

Enos Slaughter, of the Yankees, and Gil Hodges, of the Dodgers cross swords prior to Game 2 of the 1955 World Series.

York in '51 and in San Francisco in '62—but the Yankees kept coming back to their most familiar October foe.

In '63, the Dodgers swept the Yankees behind superior pitching. Podres looked as comfortable as he had in '55, taking a shutout into the ninth inning at Yankee Stadium in his 4–1 victory in Game 2.

The Yankees would score only four runs in the Series, beaten twice by Sandy Koufax, who had been a teenage bit player on the '55 team. They fared a little better against the Cardinals in the '64 Series, extending it to seven games before losing, but the years that followed would be largely barren for the Yankees.

As the Yankees sunk to sixth place in 1965 and 10th the next season, the Dodgers were winning two more pennants and the '65 Series. But arthritis forced Koufax into early retirement after the '66 season, and the Dodgers did not return to the Fall Classic until 1974.

They lost to Oakland that season and returned in 1977. The site? Yankee Stadium, of course. Three of the next five World Series would feature the Yankees and the Dodgers.

In '77, Reggie Jackson's three-homer game clinched the title for the Yankees in Game 6 in the Bronx. In Game 2 of the '78 Series, Jackson had another chance to star. There were two runners on with two outs in the top of the ninth inning at Dodger Stadium. Jackson fouled off three pitches with two strikes, running the count full against the hard-throwing rookie right-hander, Bob Welch. When Welch blew his fastball past Jackson for strike three, the Dodgers had taken a 2–0 lead in the Series.

But the Yankees would never lose again. It was as if the Dodgers had a "B" on their caps again. Back in New York for Game 3, everything came up Yankees. Graig Nettles put on a show at third base, robbing the Dodgers repeatedly with diving catches. Cy Young winner Ron Guidry gave up seven walks in a complete game, but only one run.

In Game 4, Jackson prevented what could have been a crushing double play with a turn of his hip. Camped between first and second base, Jackson let a throw by Bill Russell glance off his hip as a run scored on the play. The Yankees would win by a run.

The Yankees' 18-hit barrage in Game 5 brought them back to L.A. for the clincher, a 7–2 victory by Catfish Hunter. The Dodgers would have to wait three years for their

revenge, and they got it with a six-game victory in the 1981 World Series.

This time, it was the Yankees who won the first two at home and then dropped four straight. Owner George Steinbrenner could not handle the defeat, brawling with a fan in the elevator of the team's hotel in Los Angeles, and then issuing a public apology after the Yankees dropped the Series.

Steinbrenner never forgave his prize free agent, Dave Winfield, for going 1-for-22 in the Series. But he also never realized how good he had it simply by reaching the World Series that season.

When the Dodgers returned to the Series in 1988, the Yankees finished fifth. And when the Yankees resumed making regular trips to the Series in 1996, the Dodgers were still searching for their way back.

Red Sox

It was a sight no one ever expected: the Boston Red Sox celebrating at Yankee Stadium, taking over the old ballpark, whooping and hollering on the field, deep into the night after Game 7 of the 2004 American League Championship Series.

Surveying the scene from the loge level, Yankees owner George Steinbrenner ordered that the Red Sox be allowed to celebrate for as long as they wanted. The lights stayed on. The Curse of the Bambino, the Yankees' cosmic hold over their rivals for more than 80 years, had expired.

"There's no curse," said Jason Varitek, the Red Sox catcher, drenched in champagne that night. "The curse, in my opinion, was just being outplayed. That team outplayed us over the years."

As understatements go, that would rank high. The Yankees had outplayed all of baseball since 1920, but no team felt the sting of their domination more than the Red Sox. They are close in proximity, familiar on the field and haunted by the sense that they inspired the Yankees' glory.

Consider that before Jan. 3, 1920, the Yankees had never finished in first place. The Red Sox had won five World Series, the most of any team. The Yankees' closest brush came in 1904, when they were known as the Highlanders. They lost to the Boston Pilgrims—as the Red Sox were then known—on a wild pitch in the final game, giving Boston the AL pennant.

But everything would change on that fateful

January day when the Yankees bought Babe Ruth from the Red Sox. Starting then, the Yankees won 26 championships before the Red Sox captured another.

Boston finally did it in 2004, following a historic ALCS victory with a four-game sweep of the St. Louis Cardinals in the World Series. The Cardinal who made the last out, Edgar Renteria, was wearing a number that resonated in New England: 3, Ruth's number for the Yankees.

Red Sox owner Harry Frazee had sold Ruth for $125,000 and a $350,000 loan against the mortgage of Fenway Park. Explaining himself in *The New York Times*, Frazee said the Red Sox "were fast becoming a one-man team." It was a pitiful excuse.

Ruth had helped carry the Red Sox to the 1915, 1916 and 1918 World Series titles, and he simply cost too much for Frazee, who years later financed a Broadway play called "No, No, Nanette" that is often cited as the reason he sold Ruth. Frazee got his cash, and the Yankees got Ruth's karma.

Ruth led the Yankees to seven pennants, winning four titles and batting .347 for the Yankees in the World Series. He ushered in the

Yankees' arrival as the premier sports franchise in the world, and doomed the Red Sox to decades of heartbreak.

When the Yankees christened Yankee Stadium on April 18, 1923, the Red Sox were there. Frazee, who lived in New York, even sat with the Yankees' owner, Col. Jacob Ruppert, at the game. With some 74,200 other fans crowding the park, Ruth slammed the first home run and the Yankees won, 4–1.

The Yankees would finish the season as world champions for the first time, and the Red Sox had basically given them the title. Ruth was one of 11 players on the 1923 World Series roster who had previously played for Boston. Four of the Yankees' starting pitchers—Joe Bush, Waite Hoyt, Sam Jones and Herb Pennock—had been traded or sold by the Red Sox to the Yankees.

The Red Sox finished last that season and would stay in the cellar from 1924 through 1930. That May, they sold pitcher Red Ruffing to the Yankees, only to see him turn into a Hall of Famer, as Hoyt and Pennock were also doing.

It was not until the late 1930s that the Red Sox recovered, but even then, the Yankees never let them get too close. Boston finished

Joe DiMaggio chats with his brother Dom, of the Boston Red Sox, before a game at Yankee Stadium, 1942.

Icons of their era: Ted Williams and Mickey Mantle at Fenway Park in Boston, circa 1955.

second to the Yankees in 1938, 1939, 1941 and 1942, but the Yankees won the pennant by at least nine games each time.

By then, an individual rivalry raged within the teams' rivalry. The careers of Joe DiMaggio and Ted Williams, two California prodigies who became the preeminent hitters of the era, overlapped for 10 years.

In '41, when Williams hit .406, he did not even win the MVP award. DiMaggio won it, having fashioned his famous 56-game hitting streak the same year. The stately DiMaggio, older by about four years, preferred to stand apart from the hotheaded Williams.

"Joe resented all comparisons to Williams, whom he thought of as a brat—Teddy Tantrum," wrote Richard Ben Cramer in his biography of DiMaggio, *The Hero's Life*.

Both players missed three years to World War II, and the Red Sox won the pennant in '46, the Yankees in '47. Boston then lost the pennant on the final day of the season in two successive years: to Cleveland in 1948 and to the Yankees in '49.

The Red Sox played at Yankee Stadium for the final two games of that season, needing one victory to reach the World Series. But

Johnny Lindell's eighth-inning homer gave the Yankees a 5–4 win in the first game, and Vic Raschi's complete game, 5–3 victory clinched the pennant the next day.

The '49 season began a stretch of 17 consecutive years in which the Yankees finished ahead of the Red Sox in the standings. But the Yankees were shells of themselves by the mid-1960s, and in '66 they landed in the basement, a half-game behind Boston.

While the Red Sox rose to first in '67, the Yankees lost 90 games. When the Red Sox reached the World Series again, in 1975, the Yankees finished 12 games back in the AL East.

But the Red Sox had a core of young talent that would keep the team competitive for several years, and the Yankees were discovering the joys of free agency. They added Catfish Hunter in '75 and Reggie Jackson in '77 and had also picked up reliever Sparky Lyle, the 1977 AL Cy Young winner, in a 1972 trade with the Red Sox for journeyman first baseman Danny Cater.

After reaching the World Series twice in a row, the Yankees fell 14 games behind the Red Sox by July 19, 1978. But by the morning of Sept. 7, the lead was down to four, with the teams set to face each other in a four-game showdown at Fenway Park.

The Yankees swept, convincingly—the scores were 15–2, 13–2, 7–0 and 7–4—and they surged ahead by 3½ games on Sept. 16 after Hunter beat the Red Sox at the Stadium. Boston would win 12 of its last 14 to force a one-game playoff at Fenway on Oct. 2, Mike Torrez against Ron Guidry.

That, of course, was the game Bucky Dent popped a go-ahead three-run homer over the Green Monster in the seventh inning. It earned Dent an expletive for a middle name whenever he returned to Boston, where the Red Sox nursed that defeat for decades.

Through 2005, the Red Sox had finished second to the Yankees in the AL East for eight consecutive seasons. It was the longest streak in major league history of clubs finishing 1-2 atop the standings. But the introduction of the wild card for the 1995 postseason set up three delicious ALCS matchups between the old rivals.

The first came in 1999, in the middle of the Yankees' three-title run at the close of the century. Bernie Williams' walk-off homer to center off Rod Beck won Game 1, and the Yankees took the series handily, four games to one.

There were subtle signs that the rivalry would reach a crescendo again, memorable moments on and off the field. In 2001, Boston's Carl Everett broke up a perfect-game bid by Mike Mussina with two outs and two strikes in the ninth inning at Fenway.

The next offseason, after the Yankees outbid the Red Sox to sign Cuban righty Jose Contreras, Red Sox president Larry Lucchino dubbed the Yankees "the evil empire" in an interview with Murray Chass of *The New York Times*.

In 2003, the teams met in the ALCS, brawling in the third game at Fenway Park, when Pedro Martinez tossed a charging Don Zimmer, the 72-year-old Yankees bench coach, to the ground in the melee. Roger Clemens won that game, but he had nothing in Game 7 at Yankee Stadium and needed Mussina to bail him out of a first-and-third, no-out jam in the fourth inning.

Mussina did that, but the Yankees still trailed by 4–0. Two solo homers by Jason Giambi brought them closer, and it was 5–2 Boston in the eighth inning, with the pennant five outs away. Martinez gave up two hits and a run, and Red Sox Manager Grady Little infamously stuck with him.

It was a decision that cost Little his job.

Two doubles, by Hideki Matsui and Jorge Posada, tied the score, 5-5, and Aaron Boone's leadoff homer off Tim Wakefield's first pitch of the bottom of the 11th inning won the series for New York. Mariano Rivera, who blanked Boston for three innings of relief in Game 7, was the Series MVP.

The next season included the Yankees' thrilling 5–4 victory in 13 innings on July 1 in the Bronx, the night Derek Jeter bloodied his face while making a critical catch in the stands in the 12th inning. In September, after another crushing loss to the Yankees, Martinez confessed, "I just tip my hat and call the Yankees my daddy."

On Oct. 16, the Yankees humbled the Red Sox, 19–8, to take a 3–0 lead in the ALCS. On the morning of Game 4, the First Baptist Church near Fenway offered this topic for Sunday worship: "Why Does God Allow Suffering?" It seemed like a painfully appropriate sermon for Red Sox fans.

But on their way to another gloomy winter, the Red Sox rallied in the ninth inning off Rivera. They tied the game on a walk by Kevin Millar, a stolen base by pinch-runner Dave Roberts and a single by Bill Mueller. They won it in 12 on a homer by David Ortiz, who won Game 5 the next day with a single in the 14th.

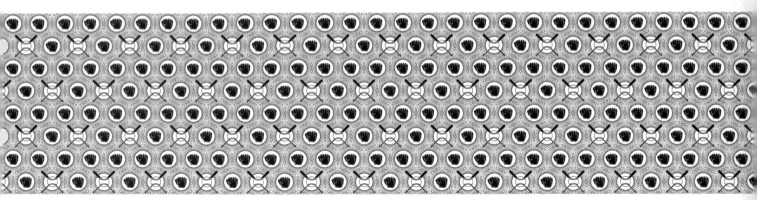

Curt Schilling, with blood seeping through his right sock as he pitched through a severe ankle injury, beat the Yankees in Game 6 at Yankee Stadium. Alex Rodriguez—the star who had almost come to Boston in a trade the previous winter—exemplified the Yankees' desperation, illegally slapping a ball from Bronson Arroyo's glove on a tag play in the eighth inning.

The next night was all Boston. The Yankees had run out of reliable starters, and Kevin Brown had nothing. Series MVP David Ortiz hit one of four Boston homers, all pulled to right field, just where The Babe used to hit them. Johnny Damon's grand slam in the second, off Javier Vazquez, was the crusher.

After so many decades of torment, maybe the Red Sox had to do it the hard way. They became the first team in baseball history to win a postseason series after trailing three games to none.

"Nothing happens easily for the Red Sox," Damon said, least of all a triumph over the New York Yankees.

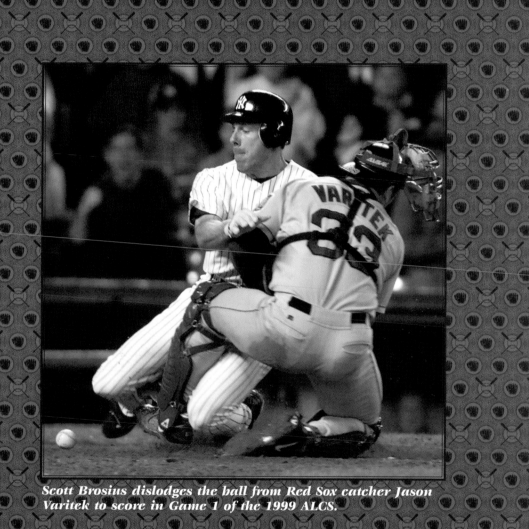

Scott Brosius dislodges the ball from Red Sox catcher Jason Varitek to score in Game 1 of the 1999 ALCS.

Bill Dickey

FACTS AND FIGURES

Retired Numbers

No.	PLAYER	No.	PLAYER
1	Billy Martin	10	Phil Rizzuto
3	Babe Ruth	15	Thurman Munson
4	Lou Gehrig	16	Whitey Ford
5	Joe DiMaggio	23	Don Mattingly
7	Mickey Mantle	32	Elston Howard
8	Yogi Berra	42	Jackie Robinson*
8	Bill Dickey	44	Reggie Jackson
9	Roger Maris	49	Ron Guidry

MVPs

PLAYER	YEAR	PLAYER	YEAR
Alex Rodriguez	2005	Yogi Berra	1951
Don Mattingly	1985	Phil Rizzuto	1950
Thurman Munson	1976	Joe DiMaggio	1947
Elston Howard	1963	Spud Chandler	1943
Mickey Mantle	1962	Joe Gordon	1942
Roger Maris	1961	Joe DiMaggio	1941
Roger Maris	1960	Joe DiMaggio	1939
Mickey Mantle	1957	Lou Gehrig	1936
Mickey Mantle	1956	Lou Gehrig	1927
Yogi Berra	1955	Babe Ruth	1923
Yogi Berra	1954		

Triple Crown

PLAYER	YEAR
Mickey Mantle	1956
Lou Gehrig	1934

Whitey Ford

Rookies
— of the Year —

PLAYER	YEAR
Derek Jeter	1996
Dave Righetti	1981
Thurman Munson	1970
Stan Bahnsen	1968
Tom Tresh	1962
Tony Kubek	1957
Bob Grim	1954

Cy Young
— Award Winners —

PLAYER	YEAR
Roger Clemens	2001
Ron Guidry	1978
Sparky Lyle	1977
Whitey Ford	1961
Bob Turley	1958

Yankees Statistical Leaders
CAREER

BATTING AVERAGE

RANK	PLAYER	AVG
1.	Babe Ruth	.349
2.	Lou Gehrig	.340
3.	Earle Combs	.325
4.	Joe DiMaggio	.325
5.	Derek Jeter	.314

HOME RUNS

RANK	PLAYER	HRs
1.	Babe Ruth	659
2.	Mickey Mantle	536
3.	Lou Gehrig	493
4.	Joe DiMaggio	361
5.	Yogi Berra	358

RBIs

RANK	PLAYER	RBIs
1.	Lou Gehrig	1,995
2.	Babe Ruth	1,971
3.	Joe DiMaggio	1,537
4.	Mickey Mantle	1,509
5.	Yogi Berra	1,430

RUNS

RANK	PLAYER	RUNS
1.	Babe Ruth	1,959
2.	Lou Gehrig	1,888
3.	Mickey Mantle	1,677
4.	Joe DiMaggio	1,390
5.	Bernie Williams	1,301

STOLEN BASES

RANK	PLAYER	SBs
1.	Rickey Henderson	326
2.	Willie Randolph	251
3.	Hal Chase	248
4.	Roy White	233
5.	Derek Jeter	215

SLUGGING

RANK	PLAYER	PCT.
1.	Babe Ruth	.711
2.	Lou Gehrig	.632
3.	Joe DiMaggio	.579
4.	Mickey Mantle	.557
5.	Jason Giambi	.529

OPS

RANK	PLAYER	PCT.
1.	Babe Ruth	1.195
2.	Lou Gehrig	1.080
3.	Mickey Mantle	.977
4.	Joe DiMaggio	.977
5.	Jason Giambi	.945

GAMES

RANK	PLAYER	GAMES
1.	Mickey Mantle	2,401
2.	Lou Gehrig	2,164
3.	Yogi Berra	2,116
4.	Babe Ruth	2,084
5.	Bernie Williams	1,945

WINS

RANK	PLAYER	WINs
1.	Whitey Ford	236
2.	Red Ruffing	231
3.	Lefty Gomez	189
4.	Ron Guidry	170
5.	Bob Shawkey	168

ERA

RANK	PLAYER	ERA
1.	Mariano Rivera	2.33
2.	Russ Ford	2.54
3.	Jack Chesbro	2.58
4.	Al Orth	2.72
5.	Tiny Bonham	2.73

STRIKEOUTS

RANK	PLAYER	Ks
1.	Whitey Ford	1,956
2.	Ron Guidry	1,778
3.	Red Ruffing	1,526
4.	Lefty Gomez	1,468
5.	Andy Pettitte	1,275

SAVES

RANK	PLAYER	SAVES
1.	Mariano Rivera	379
2.	Dave Righetti	224
3.	Goose Gossage	151
4.	Sparky Lyle	141
5.	Johnny Murphy	104

Stars of '61: Roger Maris and Mickey Mantle

Yankees Statistical Leaders
SINGLE SEASON

BATTING AVG

RANK	PLAYER	AVG	YEAR
1.	Babe Ruth	.393	1923
2.	Joe DiMaggio	.381	1939
3.	Lou Gehrig	.379	1930
4.	Babe Ruth	.378	1924
5.	Babe Ruth	.378	1921

HOME RUNS

RANK	PLAYER	HR	YEAR
1.	Roger Maris	61	1961
2.	Babe Ruth	60	1927
3.	Babe Ruth	59	1921
4.	Mickey Mantle	54	1961
	Babe Ruth	54	1920
	Babe Ruth	54	1928

RBIs

RANK	PLAYER	RBIs	YEAR
1.	Lou Gehrig	184	1931
2.	Lou Gehrig	175	1927
3.	Lou Gehrig	174	1930
4.	Babe Ruth	171	1921
5.	Joe DiMaggio	167	1937

RUNS

RANK	PLAYER	RUNS	YEAR
1.	Babe Ruth	177	1921
2.	Lou Gehrig	167	1936
3.	Lou Gehrig	163	1931
	Babe Ruth	163	1928
5.	Babe Ruth	158	1920
	Babe Ruth	158	1927

STOLEN BASES

RANK	PLAYER	SBs	YEAR
1.	Rickey Henderson	93	1988
2.	Rickey Henderson	87	1986
3.	Rickey Henderson	80	1985
4.	Fritz Maisel	74	1914
5.	Ben Chapman	61	1931

SLUGGING

RANK	PLAYER	PCT	YEAR
1.	Babe Ruth	.847	1920
2.	Babe Ruth	.846	1921
3.	Babe Ruth	.772	1927
4.	Lou Gehrig	.765	1927
5.	Babe Ruth	.764	1923

OPS

RANK	PLAYER	PCT	YEAR
1.	Babe Ruth	1.379	1920
2.	Babe Ruth	1.359	1921
3.	Babe Ruth	1.309	1923
4.	Babe Ruth	1.258	1927
5.	Babe Ruth	1.253	1926

ERA

RANK	PLAYER	PCT	YEAR
1.	Spud Chandler	1.64	1943
2.	Russ Ford	1.65	1910
3.	Ron Guidry	1.74	1978
4.	Jack Chesbro	1.82	1904
5.	Hippo Vaughn	1.83	1910

WINS

RANK	PLAYER	WINS	YEAR
1.	Jack Chesbro	41	1904
2.	Carl Mays	27	1921
	Al Orth	27	1906
4.	Joe Bush	26	1922
	Russ Ford	26	1910
	Lefty Gomez	26	1934
	Carl Mays	26	1920
	Joe McGinnity	26	1901

STRIKEOUTS

RANK	PLAYER	Ks	YEAR
1.	Ron Guidry	248	1978
2.	Jack Chesbro	239	1904
3.	David Cone	222	1997
4.	Melido Perez	218	1992
5.	Al Downing	217	1964

SAVES

RANK	PLAYER	SAVES	YEAR
1.	Mariano Rivera	53	2004
2.	Mariano Rivera	50	2001
3.	Dave Righetti	46	1986
4.	Mariano Rivera	45	1999
5.	Mariano Rivera	43	1997
	Mariano Rivera	43	2005
	John Wetteland	43	1996

Year-by-Year Results

YEAR	W	L	PCT	GB	MANAGER
2005	95	67	.586	-	Joe Torre
2004	101	61	.623	-	Joe Torre
2003	101	61	.623	-	Joe Torre
2002	103	58	.640	-	Joe Torre
2001	95	65	.594	-	Joe Torre
2000	87	74	.540	-	Joe Torre
1999	98	64	.605	-	Joe Torre
1998	114	48	.704	-	Joe Torre
1997	96	66	.593	2.0	Joe Torre
1996	92	70	.568	-	Joe Torre
1995	79	65	.549	7.0	Buck Showalter
1994	70	43	.619	-	Buck Showalter
1993	88	74	.543	7.0	Buck Showalter
1992	76	86	.469	20.0	Buck Showalter
1991	71	91	.438	20.0	Stump Merrill
1990	67	95	.414	21.0	Bucky Dent-Stump Merrill
1989	74	87	.460	14.5	Dallas Green-Bucky Dent
1988	85	76	.528	3.5	Billy Martin-Lou Piniella
1987	89	73	.549	9.0	Lou Piniella
1986	90	72	.556	5.5	Lou Piniella
1985	97	64	.602	2.0	Yogi Berra-Billy Martin
1984	87	75	.537	17.0	Yogi Berra
1983	91	71	.562	7.0	Billy Martin
1982	79	83	.488	16.0	Bob Lemon-Gene Michael-Clyde King

FACTS AND FIGURES

YEAR	W	L	PCT	GB	MANAGER
1981	59	48	.551	2.0	Gene Michael-Bob Lemon
1980	103	59	.636	-	Dick Howser
1979	89	71	.556	13.5	Bob Lemon-Billy Martin
1978	100	63	.613	-	Billy Martin-Bob Lemon
1977	100	62	.617	-	Billy Martin
1976	97	62	.610	-	Billy Martin
1975	83	77	.519	12.0	Bill Virdon-Billy Martin
1974	89	73	.549	2.0	Bill Virdon
1973	80	82	.494	17.0	Ralph Houk
1972	79	76	.510	6.5	Ralph Houk
1971	82	80	.506	21.0	Ralph Houk
1970	93	69	.574	15.0	Ralph Houk
1969	80	81	.497	28.5	Ralph Houk
1968	83	79	.512	20.0	Ralph Houk
1967	72	90	.444	20.0	Ralph Houk
1966	70	89	.440	26.5	Johnny Keane-Ralph Houk
1965	77	85	.475	25.0	Johnny Keane
1964	99	63	.611	-	Yogi Berra
1963	104	57	.646	-	Ralph Houk
1962	96	66	.593	-	Ralph Houk
1961	109	53	.673	-	Ralph Houk
1960	97	57	.630	-	Casey Stengel
1959	79	75	.513	15.0	Casey Stengel
1958	92	62	.597	-	Casey Stengel
1957	98	56	.636	-	Casey Stengel
1956	97	57	.630	-	Casey Stengel
1955	96	58	.623	-	Casey Stengel

YEAR	W	L	PCT	GB	MANAGER
1954	103	51	.669	8.0	Casey Stengel
1953	99	52	.656	-	Casey Stengel
1952	95	59	.617	-	Casey Stengel
1951	98	56	.636	-	Casey Stengel
1950	98	56	.636	-	Casey Stengel
1949	97	57	.630	-	Casey Stengel
1948	94	60	.610	2.5	Bucky Harris
1947	97	57	.630	-	Bucky Harris
1946	87	67	.565	17.0	Joe McCarthy-Bill Dickey-Johnny Neun
1945	81	71	.533	6.5	Joe McCarthy
1944	83	71	.539	6.0	Joe McCarthy
1943	98	56	.636	-	Joe McCarthy
1942	103	51	.669	-	Joe McCarthy
1941	101	53	.656	-	Joe McCarthy
1940	88	66	.571	2.0	Joe McCarthy
1939	106	45	.702	-	Joe McCarthy
1938	99	53	.651	-	Joe McCarthy
1937	102	52	.662	-	Joe McCarthy
1936	102	51	.667	-	Joe McCarthy
1935	89	60	.597	3.0	Joe McCarthy
1934	94	60	.610	7.0	Joe McCarthy
1933	91	59	.607	7.0	Joe McCarthy
1932	107	47	.695	-	Joe McCarthy
1931	94	59	.614	13.5	Joe McCarthy
1930	86	68	.558	16.0	Bob Shawkey
1929	88	66	.571	18.0	Miller Huggins-Art Fletcher
1928	101	53	.656	-	Miller Huggins

FACTS AND FIGURES

YEAR	W	L	PCT	GB	MANAGER
1927	110	44	.714	-	Miller Huggins
1926	91	63	.591	-	Miller Huggins
1925	69	85	.448	28.5	Miller Huggins
1924	89	63	.586	2.0	Miller Huggins
1923	98	54	.645	-	Miller Huggins
1922	94	60	.610	-	Miller Huggins
1921	98	55	.641	-	Miller Huggins
1920	95	59	.617	3.0	Miller Huggins
1919	80	59	.576	7.5	Miller Huggins
1918	60	63	.488	13.5	Miller Huggins
1917	71	82	.464	28.5	William Donovan
1916	80	74	.519	11.0	William Donovan
1915	69	83	.454	32.5	William Donovan
1914	70	84	.455	30.0	Frank Chance-Roger Peckinpaugh
1913	57	94	.377	38.0	Frank Chance
1912	50	102	.329	55.0	Harry Wolverton
1911	76	76	.500	25.5	Hal Chase
1910	88	63	.583	14.5	George Stallings-Hal Chase
1909	74	77	.490	23.5	George Stallings
1908	51	103	.331	39.5	Clark Griffith-Norm Elberfeld
1907	70	78	.473	21.0	Clark Griffith
1906	90	61	.596	3.0	Clark Griffith
1905	71	78	.477	21.5	Clark Griffith
1904	92	59	.609	1.5	Clark Griffith
1903	72	62	.537	17.0	Clark Griffith
1902*	50	88	.362	34.0	John McGraw-Wilbert Robinson
1901*	68	65	.511	13.5	John McGraw

* Baltimore Orioles